Makeup *Lessons*

A Testimony of Prayer, Healing and Redemption at the Makeup Counter.

Peggy Frazier O'Connor

Carpenter's Son Publishing

Makeup Lessons: A Testimony of Prayer, Healing and Redemption at the Makeup Counter

Published by Carpenter's Son Publishing, Franklin, Tennessee

Published in association with Larry Carpenter of Christian Book Services, LLC
www.christianbookservices.com

Cover design by Terresa Harris, www.thisisthatgraphics.com

Cover and Interior Layout by Suzanne Lawing

Edited by Andrew Toy and James O'Connor

Printed in the United States of America

978-1-940262-40-6

Follow the author on Twitter @producerpeg

Follow us on Facebook at MakeupLessonsTheBook

Dedication

To the memory of my loving parents, Taylor and Effie,
to my husband who believes in me,
to my three children whom I love always,
and to the women and men who inspired this book.

For I am convinced that neither death nor life, neither angels nor demons, neither the present nor the future, nor any powers, neither height nor depth, nor anything else in all creation, will be able to separate us from the love of God that is in Christ Jesus our Lord.

(NIV: Romans 8:38-39)

7/30/21

To Tina ~

May God richly bless you – now and always!

Peggy Lee Frazier Morales O'Connor

Contents

Makeup Lessons

Preface

What does it mean to be blessed? I once heard Bishop T.D. Jakes define "being blessed" as the ability to overcome any adversity that life presents. In this sense, I had a very blessed childhood. My father was sick with Lupus from the time I was five years old until he passed away when I was sixteen. My mother and I not only supported him as he pursued his calling to preach by bathing and dressing him when he could barely get out of bed, but also sang with him in the Frazier Family Trio. It was a challenging life. We were never wealthy, but I had rich experiences traveling around the country and performing with my parents. I witnessed miracle after miracle during these years – healing, provision, and angels making a way for us to get to our destination. I would never trade my childhood for anything. Yes, I was blessed as a child.

My adult life has been equally "blessed", as I have had to overcome many of the challenges common for women today, including divorce, single motherhood, custody battles, long-term care-giving, remarriage, death of loved ones, and debt. When I reached the age of fifty, I was finally putting the heartache and disappointment behind me. I was working as a producer and thought I was close to achieving some professional milestones and financial security. I suffered yet another setback, however, which made it necessary for me to go back to working in retail in order to pay my bills. I was desperately seeking God. "Father, I know that You hear my prayers! I know You care about me. Please show me how to reinvent my life." Well, God answered me in so many sweet, yet unpredictable ways.

This book begins with a condensed history of my journey in life, and creates a context for the interactions I had with my clients and co-workers at the makeup counter in a major department store. I would come home night after night and share my remarkable encounters at work with my husband. He was so moved by these stories, and persistent, that he finally convinced me to write this book. Each chapter is like a parable in the Bible. The stories are short with relatable characters in an unexpected, everyday setting. Each contains a compelling message. Hence, I call each chapter a lesson.

Most lessons include multiple biblical references, making this book an interesting companion for a Bible study. Every lesson demonstrates the transformational power of earnest and heartfelt prayer. Prayer is the foundation for the spiritual makeup lessons in every situation described. The connection to the physical makeovers I provide working as a makeup consultant gave me the inspiration for the book's title – Makeup Lessons.

Because each story is based on true events, I have changed names and facts to protect the identity of my coworkers and clients. I also conceal the identity of the major department store where I worked by referring to it as MDS (Major Department Store).

Several people have assisted me in the final creation of this book by reading early versions and giving me invaluable feedback. I wish to express my gratitude to Jim O'Connor, Carol O'Connor, Robyn Schrager, Judy McGinnis and Pastor Randy Cripps.

I am also grateful to Donna Skell, Executive Director of Roaring Lambs Ministries, for her encouragement and guidance in the process of publishing my first book.

I want to thank also the important people in my life that stood by me during the darkest moments, including Patsy McDaniel, Douglas Dunn, Dorothy Conley, Evelyn Higgins, Connie Jenkins, Sharon Braxton, Bill Lewis, and Deborah Key. I will never forget my sweet Aunt Jackie, who was my greatest champion. Finally, I am grateful to my pastor, Mike Hayes, whose anointed teaching kept me anchored in the grace of Jesus Christ.

I hope these lessons will lead you to a spiritual makeover and encourage you to seek God, as well as to trust and delight in the Lord. Use the prayers at the end of each chapter and make them your own. At the same time, there is a panel after each prayer with practical lessons about skincare and makeup. I draw upon the years of experience I have selling multiple prestige cosmetic lines, including Elizabeth Arden, Lancôme, Mary Kay, and Merle Norman. My experience as a makeup consultant reveals to me that many women are confused about cosmetics. My goal is to give enough information that you can approach a makeup consultant with confidence to get the answers and products you seek. An education in proper skincare can save your life. A makeover can do wonders to lift the spirit. Treat yourself once in a while, and praise Him in all things.

Lesson #1

Praise Him in All Things

The klieg lights reflected off the soaking mist rising hundreds of feet into the air above the bottom of the thundering Niagara Falls. Spanning the falls approximately one quarter mile from the American side to the Canadian side was a steel cable set up for the purpose of demonstrating one man's goal to cross it without falling. "Thank you, Father. I praise you, Lord. I am so blessed. I love you, Jesus," were the words he uttered with every step on the slippery, sloping two-inch wide tightrope. On June 16, 2012, Nik Walenda crossed the Falls to inspire the world with his message: "Pursue your dreams. Never give up. Focus on the other side."

I missed seeing this extraordinary feat on television because I was working late that night. I finished my shift at ten o'clock. Driving home slowly, I was weeping as devastating memories replayed in my mind. I had recently gone back to work in the cosmetics department at MDS, where I had worked thirteen years ago selling fine jewelry. Once again I saw myself navigating my way through a contentious divorce while desperately trying to take care of my three children, my terminally ill mother, my disabled aunt, and myself. In the divorce decree the judge ordered the sale of our new expensive home, which my husband and I had recently purchased before he filed. We had been married twenty years. There was no possible way for me to afford that house on my income alone. As an act of faith, and to show my children that we could rely on God for our future, I decided to have a final blowout party. Two weeks later I had to move all six of us, plus two Pekingese dogs, into a seventeen hundred square foot apartment. It wasn't easy, but I did the best I could.

In 2003, God brought me a new husband, Jim. Over the next few years our love and relationship grew even as we weathered many challenges which threatened to divide us, including underemployment, blending a family, and custody battles. We believed that our marriage was worth the effort, recognizing that his strengths compensated for my weaknesses, just as my strengths compensated for his.

The beginning of our marriage was full of joy and expectation, but only three weeks after our wedding my mother died of metastasized cancer. I remember waking up in the mornings torn with conflicting emotions. On the one hand, I felt the thrill of being a newlywed. On the other hand, I also suffered the agonizing loss of my mother. She was my best friend.

The family I had tried so hard to keep together seemed to be unraveling like an old sweater. Before the wedding, my son chose to live with his father. My older daughter had just turned twenty and decided to move out and follow her own path, despite my explicit warnings and fears for her well-being. In addition, my husband's two daughters were becoming distant emotionally. Jim and I met roughly two years after we were both divorced. Before we married, I spent fourteen months developing a warm relationship with his daughters, who clearly adored their father as much as he adored them. Soon after we married, however, the girls made it clear that they preferred their mother's newly blended family over ours. Unfortunately, they also rejected my husband's extended family, which broke our hearts. Thus, out of the seven family members who came together to celebrate our wedding, only two came to live with Jim and me – Aunt Jackie and my middle daughter.

Aunt Jackie lived with my parents before I was born. She helped my mother take care of me as a child. My entire life Jackie never lived away from my mother and me. Even after I married and started a family, she came to live with us. She had no one else to care for her. Jackie was chronically ill her whole life, eventually filing for disability in 1977. By the time Jim and I married, her osteoporosis was so severe that she had a hunched back and very brittle bones. She lived in constant, debilitating pain. Having always known her as a loving and gentle soul, in spite of her challenges, I struggled to cope with the transformation in her behavior and personality, which started soon after my mother died. I didn't understand that she was in the beginning stages of dementia. She exhibited symptoms of memory loss, confusion, and combativeness. Her loss of coordination due to amputated toes caused her to fall frequently. She was tormented by unwarranted suspicions, uncharacteristic rage, moodiness and urinary incontinence. Particularly frightening was when she would overmedicate herself and write hot checks. When I would confiscate her things to protect her, she would hurl horrible insults and accusations. My sweet Aunt Jackie had always been my greatest champion and ally. To my sorrow, I had become the "enemy" in her eyes as I attempted to take care of her and keep her safe.

As time went on, we experienced several terrifying episodes where Aunt Jackie left the house and walked the streets aimlessly until some stranger brought her home. One time she fell in the street breaking her arm. Another time she climbed on the kitchen counter, fell, and broke her hip. The subsequent hip replacement surgery was considered life-threatening because she had developed two aneurisms. Any surgery could be fatal. In her mind, she was as independent and self-reliant as she was in her twenties. She had no awareness of the danger she represented to herself. Her doctor at the Senior Care Center found a place for her in a Medicaid nursing home. Moving her there made her furious. Even though I had no choice in the matter, she resented me. It was painful to watch her decline over the next four years. She finally succumbed to the horrible disease of dementia in 2009.

Meanwhile, my younger daughter was refusing to go to her new school – her third new school and school district in three years. I couldn't blame her. Moving so much had left giant holes in her education. Even though I tried many times to help her by offering one-on-one tutoring, she started to believe that she could never catch up. Understandably her grades suffered. Initially, she enthusiastically embraced my offer to homeschool her, but when the books came she refused to complete her coursework. There was no way she was going to allow me or my new husband to impose any structure in her life. She told me that she wanted things to be the way they were before I remarried. She wanted a home with her grandmother, her Aunt Jackie, and her siblings. She was still grieving the divorce and loss of my mother. As Aunt Jackie's health declined, she resisted all efforts to adjust to a new family to which she believed she didn't belong.

My older daughter would periodically return home to seek help for her chronic medical condition from which she had suffered since childhood. Because she was no longer a minor, her father dropped her from his company health plan. Her pre-existing conditions made it impossible to get individual insurance that would have provided her appropriate medical care. On top of excruciating pain, she developed a cyst on her ovary that her doctor thought might be malignant. The doctor said she required surgery. She had already gone through numerous painful experimental treatments since she was twelve years old. The experience for both of us was gut-wrenching. I had already lost my mother to cancer. Was I now going to lose my first child?

During the two months it took to raise the money for the surgery, the doctor freely prescribed narcotic pain medication to help her live with the pain. The doctors wrote the prescriptions; I bought them and gave them to her believing that I was helping. She eventually became an addict. This was horrifying and shameful to her. She became angry and despondent knowing that her addiction had been facilitated by medical professionals. Thankfully, the surgery showed that the cyst was benign. After the surgery, the doctors cut her off cold turkey from her pain medication. I felt helpless watching her continue to suffer. In fact, I nearly lost her. She has battled courageously while still living with no medical solution to her long-term condition. Over time, however, she was able to beat her addiction to pain medications.

Safely sitting at a stoplight, tissue in hand, I shook my head wondering how I made it through those days when my life was a continuous nightmare. I desperately begged God to awaken me. Night after night I walked the floor wondering what brought me to that place. I had so many dreams. Looking back was like seeing myself on that tightrope trying to walk across the deadly Niagara Falls as I performed a dangerous balancing act. One misstep and I would have disappeared into the churning waters along with everyone else I was trying to hold up.

I actually grew up as a child performer. My "career" started when I was two. As a little girl, I resembled Shirley Temple. At the time, my family lived in Houston where my father was serving as an itinerant pastor. My mother had taken me to a department store to sit for an Easter portrait. Without informing my parents, the head of the department store sent a copy of my photo to a national competition for the most beautiful child in America in 1959. I won third place. My parents were shocked when they received a phone call inviting my mother and me to New York, where I appeared on *The Today Show* and *The Howdy Doody Show.*

When I was three years old, my parents realized that I could sing as they were traveling all night from Florida to New Jersey to get home for Christmas. As my father was driving, he and my mother were singing Christmas carols in order to stay awake. From the backseat, they heard me chime in singing in harmony. My mother told me that it startled my father so much that he nearly drove off the road.

I began singing publicly with my parents when I was five years old. In the summers, my parents and I would leave our home in New Jersey and tour the southern part of the United States ministering in churches. My father, Dr. Taylor Frazier, had his masters in theology and doctorate in divinity. He was an anointed theologian who would preach inspiring messages of the grace of God and a deeper walk with Christ. He was also an accomplished jazz pianist and singer. When I performed with him, he would stand me on the piano bench next to him while he accompanied me. During the next eleven years he, my mother, and I would minister as a family, eventually recording two albums featuring gospel music. I adored my father and loved this life.

The same year I started performing with my parents, the doctors diagnosed my father with Lupus, telling him he had only months to live. In 1962, doctors knew very little about this autoimmune disease. Their diagnosis was essentially a death sentence. My father suffered physically, but was determined to do what God called him to do until the day he died. God supernaturally kept him alive for the next eleven years. I believe that living on borrowed time drove him into a relationship with Christ that few people understand. His ministry reflected that. The crippling arthritis in his hands deformed his fingers, yet amazingly, he would sit at the piano and God would play through him. Forty years later people today still tell me what a spiritual experience it was to observe him perform. I saw my father pray often for other people to be healed. Many were healed, but he never was. He died when I was sixteen. His death left me spiritually confused and emotionally devastated. I was angry at God.

Three months after my father's death I auditioned for Richard Fredericks. At that time, Richard was the lead baritone of the New York City Opera. Never in my wildest dreams did I imagine that he and his wife, Judith, would become my instructors for the next four years while I also attended The American Academy of the Dramatic Arts in New York City. On my graduation day, I crossed the stage and extended my hand to alumna and "first lady of the theatre," Helen Hayes, who gave me my diploma in the Broadway theatre named after her. At age eighteen I was ready and determined to start my career in show business. I freelanced with five agents and was under contract to a personal manager, Simon Maslow, who also managed film star Faye Dunaway. Soon I began performing in soap operas, musical revues and modeling in trade shows at Madison Square Garden.

My career was taking off, but I knew that I was hurting and running from God. Then one day, on my way to an audition, I was stuck in a traffic jam on Broadway. I happened to glance at a giant billboard, which was advertising the show, *"Your Arm's Too Short to Box with God,"* in very bold type. The taxi wasn't moving, and all I could do was stare. I heard Him. Despite my rejection of Him, I couldn't deny the awareness I had of His overwhelming presence and love for me. That day I decided that I would give up my bitterness against Him for the illness and early death of my father, quit secular work and go back to my roots as a Christian concert artist. I decided to trust God again with what I could not understand and to receive His forgiveness for my rebellion. I began touring throughout the United States, giving concerts, and recording my own albums.

While I enjoyed my life on the road, I felt incomplete. I longed for a family and at age twenty-one married the son of one of my father's dearest minister friends. He and I had known each other since he was seven and I was five. After the wedding, I continued my singing career and concert performances. My husband, however, clearly struggled with being married to a woman who was in a very public form of ministry and traveled for weeks at a time. I recall once after I had given a concert, only one month after our wedding, a man asked my husband how it felt to be "Mr. Frazier", Frazier being my maiden name. While my husband appeared to be supportive publicly, privately he was conflicted. I eventually surrendered to the pressure I felt to stay home. I gave birth to our three beautiful babies in five years. Thankfully, I had the help of my mother and Aunt Jackie to raise our children.

For the next twelve years, I stopped touring and tried to play the corporate wife. I even went to work for my husband in the car business. While I truly loved him, and loved being a mother, music and ministry had always been as natural to me as breathing. From time to time I would seek opportunities to sing again. Denying that part of myself left me feeling disoriented and frequently caused arguments between my husband and me.

My husband was the parts manager at a foreign car dealership for several years. This dealership was once the flagship store for the whole country, but now was failing because of the oil crisis in the eighties. A new owner purchased the dealership out of bankruptcy and tried unsuccessfully to save the business. We limped along trying to rebuild for about two years before they finally sold off the franchises one at a time.

At one point the general manager fired the service manager and made my husband the parts and service manager in order to save a salary. My husband told me that the business was in serious trouble. He confessed to me that he knew nothing about being a service manager. Only five cars per day were coming in for service. It wasn't enough. How could they get more business? Why did the customers leave? My husband's salary was our only income. I was at home with three small children, and my mother was recovering from uterine cancer and subsequent radiation treatment. If my husband lost his job, I knew it would be devastating for our family.

Failure of the dealership seemed inevitable, and I was desperately crying out to God for a solution. I was shopping one day when a scripture came to me out of the blue: *"Call unto Me and I will answer you and show you great and mighty things, fenced in and hidden, which you do not know"* (Jeremiah 33:3). I had always thought that verse meant we were to call unto God to ask Him for spiritual insight. At that moment, I had this intuition that He was asking me to call to Him for answers to any problem we might be facing regarding anything in our lives. It was like a light bulb going off in my head. I turned the car around and went straight to the dealership and into my husband's office. I said to him, "Where are the files of the car owners from years ago?"

"Peggy, there are no cars. They've probably been sold and have new owners."

"That's ridiculous! Surely you have files for your past customers." This was the early '90s and computers were not as prevalent as they are today.

My husband hesitated. "Well, we have boxes of files on our old customers out in the shed. But there's no telling if those customers even own the cars anymore."

"Great! Get your guys to bring me those boxes. These older cars need to be serviced, and people are taking them somewhere. Why are they not coming here? Give me a desk and a phone. I'll start making calls. You don't even have to pay me. Someone's got those cars."

My husband stood there looking at me dumbstruck for a moment. Then he shrugged his shoulders as if to say, "Okay. What can it hurt? We have nothing to lose."

My hunch was right! God was directing me, and I knew it. About half the people I called still owned their cars, but didn't know that we were under new management. Those that did know, however, believed that the dealership would overcharge them for service just as the previous management had done. I politely explained that we used factory-authorized parts, not the after-market parts frequently used by independent repair shops. To show that we were different, I offered them a continental breakfast, free oil change, and a private clinic with the new technicians when they brought their car on Saturday morning. They would have the opportunity to meet my husband and the new ownership. That Saturday morning, there were over twenty cars lined up. In the first week, we had at least one hundred new customers. The owner of the dealership was so pleased that he hired me and put me in charge of customer service and special promotions. I worked beside my husband, developing a loyalty marketing program for more than a year. We were celebrating the progress, believing we had turned the corner. We did not understand that we were making the business more viable on paper to be broken apart and sold as franchises to other dealers in town. We were devastated.

On the strength of my service marketing program, however, the competing dealership in town hired both my husband and me. I repeated the same successful marketing program for their three franchises as well. Business doubled for that dealership as a result of the clinics. My reward was a demotion to a customer service representative, while the service advisors made commissions on the work I was responsible for bringing into the service department.

I saw the writing on the wall and knew that my mother and Aunt Jackie were both ill. Neither of them could continue to raise my children for me while I worked ridiculous hours in the car business across town. At least I felt that my husband had secured his position with the new dealership. I was going to have to do something else, which would bring income into the family while still being home for everyone who needed me.

My family attended the church where we were first married and I sang in the choir. Soon the youth pastor and minister of music asked me if I would assist them in the production of a massive Christmas Nativity celebration. I had never produced or directed anything in my life, but I volunteered anyway. The youth pastor had experience in technical theater, and I had experience working with actors. He and I collaborated well together along with the minister of music.

I felt as though I had been let out of prison. I found that I loved producing more than anything I had ever done. After the Christmas presentation, the youth pastor and I collaborated again to produce a dinner theater for the church. I was hooked. The youth pastor mentored me and believed in me. He saw gifts in me that I had no idea existed. I am eternally grateful to him for helping me to understand that love never requires you to be less than what God intended you to be, or to be someone you are not.

I gained so much confidence that I quit the car business and started my own non-profit organization, which trained young people in all aspects of the creative arts. This seemed to be the solution to my problem. I could work from home, still be there for my children and provide transportation to doctors for my mother and Aunt Jackie. I produced and directed more live shows with the money I earned from teaching and with several municipal grants. Our studio also featured instruction in the art of painting on silk. One of my students, Aaron Gerstler, who was previously the poster child for Muscular Dystrophy, entered his piece in a national competition sponsored by First Lady Barbara Bush commemorating the 200th anniversary of the White House. He won, and was asked to display his artwork in both the White House and the Capitol building in Austin, Texas.

My husband's response to my creative endeavors was similar to his response years before. Consequently, as with so many marriages, ours hit the rocks. Still, no one was more surprised than I. After all, he grew up as a minister's kid just as I did. We both came from intact families. I knew the damage divorce could do from my father's experience with his first wife. I often took comfort from my belief that my husband and I shared the same faith and convictions. All my attempts to rationalize why we belonged together, however, never resonated with him. He was miserable, while I was beginning to thrive.

On a Monday the week before our first separation, I got the lead in an independent film called *Unto Thee*. On Wednesday, I got a contract to be the featured soloist for the 100th anniversary celebration for the Dallas Country Club. On Friday, the district manager for a Houston car dealership called to offer me, not my husband, a contract to implement the same marketing miracle I had performed for the dealerships where my husband and I had worked. Previously, I wondered why God had given me the solution for attracting new service customers. Why didn't He give the solution to my husband? I instantly felt God answer me: "It is because you were the one who asked Me." At that moment, I realized a spiritual truth. God answers specific prayers. I was the one who was calling on Him and expecting Him to answer me. So, He did! I thought that my husband would be grateful to God and proud of me.

Instead, I believed he resented me. On Saturday, my husband told me that if I didn't give up all these wonderful opportunities and get a full-time job, he would leave me. On the advice of my pastor, I told my husband "no". I chose to star in the film and perform for the Country Club. After a six-month standoff, he agreed to go to marriage counseling with me. We went for three weeks. I have always believed and continue to maintain, that there is nothing that God cannot heal through the power of the Holy Spirit. Both people have to believe this and both people have to be willing to do the work. My husband was not interested.

I did not see him treating family life as his first priority. I stayed believing that he would get some help with me to salvage our marriage and for the sake of our children. We separated, then reconciled. I was grateful to God when it looked as though my marriage would survive, but then devastated when we separated again. Soon my marriage failed completely. During the divorce proceedings, my ex-husband explained to the judge why he was seeking a divorce: "It is just something I have to do."

After the divorce, I went to see the pastor at my church. I told him about the theological perspective of an organization which promotes the position that a spouse should remain faithful and pray for reconciliation no matter what, even if the other spouse remarries. He showed me in the Word that if an unbelieving spouse wants to stay, it is best that you also stay, as your behavior and testimony can be the necessary light that causes them to come to know Christ. If an unbeliever wants to leave, however, then you are released (1 Corinthians 7:15). I could not say where my ex-husband stood with the Lord, but he clearly did not believe in our marriage, and he had no interest at all in praying with our children and me, talking about the Lord, or attending church as a family. I finally realized that there had been no unity between my husband and me for years. At that moment, I felt the Lord release me.

After my divorce, I never felt comfortable dating or even going to singles' meetings at church. After being married for twenty years, I didn't know how to be single. I remember burying my head in my mother's lap in her room and weeping, "Mama, I don't know how to start over. I can't imagine my life without him."

My mother took my face into her hands and said, "One day, sweetheart, when you least expect it, you will turn a corner and the man who is to be your husband will be standing there."

I took her advice to mean that I should not go out searching for love. Instead, I should go about my life, and God would bring me a husband who was right for me when the time was right. Instead of letting my ex-husband be my idol, I finally closed the door on my marriage and let him go.

The stress of being a single mother, working multiple jobs and trying to be there for my mother, my aunt, and three broken-hearted children got to be too much for me to handle. Extreme stress and sleep deprivation can cause the mind to think irrationally. I noticed that not only was I having trouble remembering things, but also my hair was falling out. Years of continuous stress were soon complicated by the beginning phase of menopause. My doctor suggested that I was also suffering from adrenal exhaustion. He explained that adrenaline is a stress-producing chemical which kicks in when the body is faced with a "fight or flight" situation. Humans were never intended to live on adrenaline for extended periods of time.

I recall one particular week where I made two visits to different hospitals and once more to the emergency room. When I would come home from my full-time job selling jewelry and my part-time job as a vocal and acting coach, I was cook, chauffeur, and tutor to my children. I wanted to make life as normal as possible, so I made sure that they were able to participate in baseball, football, cheerleading, school plays and musicals. I hosted birthday parties and sleepovers. I took my kids to theme parks and movies. Aunt Jackie and my mother did so much to help me maintain equilibrium, but the stress was taking its toll on their health and emotional stability as well. I had no extended family to lean on for help, and I was the only licensed driver. My mother, who had helped me with driving in the past, was now going blind due to macular degeneration. On top of that, she was also being treated with various topical ointments for a fungal infection on her abdomen. After a year of this with no improvement, her doctor finally diagnosed her with cancer in the navel. No one had ever heard of such a thing!

I had never felt so tired in all my life. I was having trouble pulling my thoughts together, and I could not keep up the pace. The wheels were starting to come off. Even though it may have looked as though I was functioning well, I was completely terrified.

Finally, I reached a breaking point. I had just arrived at my job at MDS. I was facing eight hours on my feet. After putting the jewelry into the display cases, I felt dizzy when I stood up. Suddenly, I was overwhelmed by the belief that I couldn't take care of everyone well enough. My ex-husband would take my children, and my mother would die. I couldn't do this anymore. I believed I would ultimately fail everyone I loved. It would just be better if I killed myself. In my irrational state of mind, I started to develop a plan. I would leave my shift early to go home when I knew my children would be at school. I would leave a note, get in my car to go to an undisclosed location, and quietly take my life before they came home.

Thankfully, God had a different plan. Just as the doors were opening for the day, I saw my pastor's wife and daughter enter the store. Because I was a new member at their large church, they didn't know me or anything about my situation. I went up to greet them, and immediately burst into tears. I explained my circumstances to them, and they prayed for me. Through their prayers that morning, the Holy Spirit gave me the strength and the ability to believe that He was going to make a way for me. I did not know how, but He knew that I was desperate, and He sent the head of my church to save me. For the first time, I felt hope spring up inside me.

From that point on, God put me on a path to my healing and my future. After I quit the car business, I worked occasionally for a woman by the name of Shirley Abrams, who was an iconic casting director in Dallas, Texas. I started out as her assistant and graduated years later to her associate. Together, we cast commercials, films, and television programs. She and her daughter, Linda, became precious friends of mine. Years later, after I had remarried, Shirley had a stroke and was hospitalized. Linda called me from the hospital to say that her mother was dying and wanted to see me. It was a scene I will never forget. Shirley had refused all medical support and told me that she and Linda had wanted me to continue her business. Shirley's death hit me hard, but I was honored to conduct her memorial service for the local film community. I honored her request to continue her business by forming Abrams-O'Connor Multimedia Theatrical Casting, Inc. Shirley's casting business had dropped off dramatically due to her failing health. While she had an outstanding reputation, there were no assets in the company. Even though there was no real business to continue, I kept her name out of respect for her.

Still, I was able to land several meaningful casting jobs, including a SAG feature film project in the spring of 2006. By the time shooting started, my job was done. The director, however, invited my husband, Jim, and me to come to the set one evening as they were filming a night shoot. To keep the extras awake, they showed the classic film, "*Steel Magnolias*"(1), which features the lives of Southern women in Louisiana, who face the trials of life together with humor, grit, and determination. The central character of the movie is Shelby, played by Julia Roberts. This young woman suffers from diabetes, yet chooses to have a child anyway, which proves to be a fateful decision. After the birth of her son, she dies from kidney failure.

As I finished watching the film, I heard God speak to my spirit and say, "You know, I am the only one who can truly make a steel magnolia." That night, He told me that He wanted me to create a platform for His daughters. At that moment, the Lord birthed in me a vision for a project called,

"In Search of Steel Magnolias". I knew in my heart that God wanted me to shed light on what He was doing around the world with women of all races and cultures, who, by His power had overcome great obstacles to be shining lights in a dark world. I started to weep. I started to argue with Him. I told Him that He had the wrong girl. Moses argued with God about going back to Egypt to face Pharaoh after he had run in fear because he had killed an Egyptian. Like Moses, God was telling me that if I would just be obedient and face my fear, He would do a transforming work in me.

In the middle of the turmoil in my life, I felt nothing like a "steel magnolia". I had no clue what to do with this vision God had given me. I was trying to figure out how to run a casting company. I eventually realized that I needed to form a film company. Through a connection in New York, I landed a contract with a fledgling Internet broadcast company that coincidentally had contracts to broadcast sporting events in Texas, Louisiana, and New Jersey. They focused on sending high definition content via the Internet to computers and cellular devices. At the time, this was groundbreaking technology. Over the next three years, I was their executive producer in charge of production for sporting events in Texas, as well as concerts, military documentaries, and political programs based in Sacramento, California. I did this with the promise of equity and several hundred thousand dollars for contracted services. After all this work, the owners of the company told me that they were not successful in getting the final funding needed to launch. The company defaulted on the payments owed to me and to the crews that the company asked me to hire.

While I was producing these other projects, my vision for "In Search of Steel Magnolias" never left my heart or my mind. I wanted to produce an episodic series. Each episode would feature the life and work of a special, but unsung woman who was overcoming challenges and doing her part to build the Kingdom of God on the earth. One of my goals with the project was to create new role models for young women. While I thoroughly enjoyed being a sports and entertainment producer and living in California, I saw this work primarily as a stepping stone for launching my passion project without having to rely on investors. Why else would God have given me this opportunity in California?

When everything went belly up I remembered crying out to God, "Father, I am so sorry. I guess I missed you."

I felt Him reply, "It's all right. Stop crying! I allowed it so that you could gain the skills and experience you need to produce the project I gave you."

I kept recalling this scripture: *"All things work together and are for good to and for those who love God and are called according to His design and purpose. For those whom He foreknew, He also destined from the beginning to be molded into the image of His Son…"* (Romans 8:28-29). I finally understood that it was not my purpose, but His. He also has the way and the means to equip me for His purpose.

While God had given me a fresh vision for my life, a dream to pursue, and an opportunity to cross to the other side, there was no funding yet. After ten years of marriage with Jim, we were empty-nesters. He was working, but I had no income. It seemed that I had no other choice except to go back to work in retail. I needed a flexible schedule to work on my project, attend meetings, and move the dream into a reality. At the same time, I had to pay my bills, small as they were. How would I get to the other side working in retail?

There was no traffic at ten o'clock at night, so I arrived home from work quickly and safely. I was still weepy as I sat in my car in the garage. Before I went inside, I was doing my best to compose myself. Then as if on cue, my older daughter called me. She was so excited. She was telling me how proud she was of me. *Proud?!* How could my daughter be telling me that she is proud of me now? I had tried so hard to take care of my family. There just wasn't enough of me to go around. I ran out of resources because I tried to fix things that I just couldn't fix. I made the mistake of trying to be all things to all people, and became a victim of the tyranny of everyone else's "urgent" needs. I knew that God loved me, understood me and had compassion for me, but some of the people I loved were currently not in a position to be so merciful toward me. My perspective shifted when I heard Bishop T.D. Jakes say on his daily show, *The Potter's Touch*, "I have lived too long and been through too much, to let another broken human being define me." I took these words to heart. God defined me through the eyes of His mercy and grace. While I knew this to be true, the challenge I faced was how to pursue my dreams by working at the makeup counter.

My daughter had been watching Nik Walenda walk across Niagara Falls that night. Her words were like honey pouring out of my phone. "Mama, he had a microphone attached to him. You could hear him taking one step and then another, saying 'Thank you, Father. Praise you, God!' Mama, he literally praised his way to the other side. That's what you are doing with your life." Through many years of sorrow, my daughter had witnessed me singing to her songs of praise and worship, especially at bedtime when she was a child. I was repeating the same spiritual strategy my parents chose when they faced adversity in pursuit of their purpose.

As joyous as it was to hear my daughter speak praise over me, I was still far from reaching the other side. The first days in June 2012 were very emotional and difficult. I entered the department store to begin my work as a makeup consultant for a prestige cosmetic line. I was a sales consultant working for an hourly wage and a small commission. I was grateful for the job as it covered my expenses. I had been out of work for over a year. While the Internet broadcast company for which I had worked was still trying to find new funding, I was told nothing was forthcoming. I was fifty-five years old and broke. I felt betrayed and confused not only by my recent unemployment, but also by another bizarre and perilous experience at the end of 2011.

During a trip out of town in October, I needed to go to an emergency room for an extreme allergic reaction to something I had ingested. Through circumstances that quickly got out of my control, I found myself admitted. The doctor assigned to me was aggressively trying to treat me for conditions I did not have, so I refused all medical orders. After frustrating delays, when it was clear that my medical records had been compromised, the staff released me to go home. After my release, I sought legal counsel. My attorneys suggested to me that I was a victim of insurance fraud and medical identity theft. I found current news stories about other patients who had similar terrifying experiences with the same hospital. My attorneys advised me that I would see no vindication or compensation unless I was willing to devote resources I did not have and invest the next ten years of my life in a quixotic fight against a system that is simply bigger than I am. Was I willing for this bizarre episode to consume me? I was resigned to the only answer which seemed available to me -

"No!"

For the next seven months, I felt uncomfortable leaving my home. I was not upset or afraid, but I was thoughtful. I felt as though I was living in two dimensions. Prior to that experience, I believed that, as human beings, we have temporary spiritual experiences. I now understood that we are spiritual beings having a temporary human experience. God became a daily presence in my life. My new peaceful existence that passed all understanding was something I found difficult to articulate to others. I needed time to process the inversion of my being. When I struggled to explain it, I referred to it as sweet and sour sauce. It made no sense really, but I loved the taste.

In January of 2012, only two months after my crisis, I went on a fast in response to a challenge from my pastor. I sought the Lord for three weeks about what I was to do with the rest of my life. I laid the situation before the Lord. I believed His answer was clear. I was to give this nightmare experience to Him. He was going to deal with it. I was not to look back, but to focus on the special project that He had given me to do. He was so real to me during this time. I trusted Him implicitly with my life because He had proven Himself faithful. I knew that He would be my advocate.

During my fast, I resumed working on my passion project, "In Search of Steel Magnolias". I called my director and asked him to finish the trailer. I was hoping to use it to raise money for the project. What followed next was an experience I will never forget.

I received a Facebook friend request from a man whose name and picture I did not recognize. His name was Wayne McEntire. I ignored him at first, but soon he messaged me again. He explained that he was a young boy in the fifth grade when my parents and I came to town and held a revival service at the First Baptist Church of Westlake, Louisiana. My parents and I had been coming to the Lake Charles area to conduct such meetings for nine years. Wayne remembered that, in 1973, my father preached his last sermon in that church and then passed away in Westlake.

"I am now the pastor of First Baptist Church of Westlake where your father preached his last message," Wayne informed me.

"Really!" I replied in stunned amazement.

"Yes. I'm doing an illustrated sermon this month. I'm calling it, 'The Mountaintop Experiences of Life Which Carry You Through the Valleys.' Your father was one of my mountaintop experiences when I was in the fifth grade. I'd like to include him in my presentation. Would you have any pictures of him, your mother, and you which you could send to me?"

"Yes, I'm sure I could find some pictures and have my husband scan them for you. Would that work for you?"

"That would be perfect," Wayne replied.

My father would be so delighted to know that he had an effect on a young man who was eventually called to preach.

"Wayne, I went through a terrible ordeal a few months ago. It's brought me to a new relationship with God at this stage of my life. I want to ask you a question."

"What is it?"

"I need to make a public statement in the face of the enemy. It is not over for me until God says it is over! Would you let me come to Westlake to stand on the platform where my father preached his last message and sing?"

"Of course! We would love to have you come visit us. After thirty-nine years, it would be a great homecoming."

"Yes, it would." I continued the conversation by telling him about my passion project.

"You know, Peggy, you might be interested to know that some of the extended members of the real family behind the *Steel Magnolias* movie still attend this church."

I felt my knees go weak. "I had no idea that the film was based on a true story. I need to speak to them so that they know what I'm doing."

"You should call Marcelene Thornton. I'll email you her phone number after I get her permission to give it to you." He soon sent me an email that said Marcelene would be happy to speak to me.

I called Marcelene immediately. I was stammering. "Mi...Miss Marcelene, I am so sorry. I thought this film was a work of fiction. I'm calling you because I felt it was important for you to know what God wanted me to do..."

Marcelene stopped me in mid-sentence, "Peggy, Peggy. Don't you know who I am? You may not recognize my name because I've remarried. You used to play with my daughter when you came to Westlake with your parents. I'm Lisa's mother."

I couldn't believe it! Marcelene was Lisa Robinson's mother and the mother-in-law of Susan Robinson, the real woman behind the Julia Robert's character, Shelby, in the film. We talked for two hours or so and shared fond memories of my family and our time together in evangelism.

Two weeks later my husband, my assistant, and Sharon Braxton, the host of "In Search of Steel Magnolias," spent the weekend with Marcelene and her precious family. We even met the real "Ouiser", played by Shirley McClain in the movie. The real "Ouiser" was celebrating her 40th wedding anniversary with her husband that weekend. At Marcelene's invitation, she changed her plans and came with her husband to Westlake to meet me. Unlike the movie character, Ouiser is a vivacious, uplifting, and gracious woman of God, who now gives her testimony at women's conferences.

Words cannot adequately express the emotions I felt that day. On the one hand, I felt exhilarated to be standing and singing in the church where my father preached his last message thirty-nine years ago. On the other hand, when I looked down at the audience, I saw his casket in my mind. I knew God was bringing my life full circle from age 16 when I became angry at Him. He is the God of the second chance. He never wastes a tear or a sorrow. He collects all our tears in a bottle (Psalm 56:8).

I came home after that amazing weekend in Westlake determined to finish the website and the trailer. I was working with professionals who were willing to advance their time, but it was taking a long time to complete. I could not wait any longer. I had to get a job to pay my bills as I pursued my vision. It seemed to make sense to go back to retail. I had done this kind of work before.

The job opening at MDS was not in jewelry this time. It was in the cosmetics department. In the past I had sold cosmetics for a different company, so I knew I could do the job. In my mind, this was an acceptable compromise because I was only taking a part-time job, not starting another "career". This would allow me the flexibility to keep my passion project moving forward. I did not want to leave this world without being able to say to God that I did what I believed in my heart He had given me to do.

I had no idea that this "temporary", part-time job was part of the process God was doing in me. He was going to use this experience to redeem my past, taking me back to 1998, just as He took me back to Westlake. He was going to heal the places of sorrow in my life, and turn them for His glory. As I finished my first day, I walked slowly to my car, sat down, and wept. Feelings of confusion and failure swept over me. In view of what had happened in Westlake less than four months before, this part of my spiritual journey made no sense to me. I was poised to go forward full throttle into my future. Instead, I found myself catapulted back to a place that resurrected painful memories that I would rather forget. It seemed cruel.

I had flashbacks of my mother when I was sixteen years old, and my father had just passed away. It seemed so unfair that God would take my father from us while we were on the road. Nine times in eleven years we thought his time had come. That was most of my childhood. His physicians had repeatedly advised him to be never more than fifteen minutes from the hospital. His response was, "God did not call me to sit around and wait for death. I will die with my preaching boots on!" And that he did.

My mother and I traveled the country with him ministering as a family. His disease frequently caused sheet-soaking fevers, especially at night. These attacks would be followed by freezing chills. In the morning, we would feed him, dress him, and put him in the car. He would lie down in the backseat as we would drive from church to church all summer. At each meeting, we would lift him out of the car, point him in the direction of the pulpit and for almost two hours he would sing, play piano, and preach as though he never had a sick day in his life. It was difficult, miraculous, and supernatural. The Spirit of God moved in ways that were so powerful I felt I could touch Him.

In July of 1973, we had just arrived at First Baptist Church of Westlake, Louisiana. The revival began on Sunday. Daddy was not well at all. We had seen him much more ill in the past, but he had always rallied. This time was different. He gave his last message on Wednesday night, from a wheelchair. In the middle of the night, he woke my mother and said, "Please take me to the hospital." The last words he said to her were, "I love you. I would never have made it without you." He meant it, and it was the truth.

Saturday morning he went to be with the Lord. My mother and I drove back to Pastor Becton's house where we had been staying. We had to cross a great bridge to get from Lake Charles to Westlake. We were both sobbing. My mother cried, "Lord, I don't understand! How could you take him now? We are sixteen hundred miles away from home. I have a child, luggage, and albums, but no family to help us!" She was frightened, exhausted, and confused.

Suddenly, she stopped and began praising God. "Father, I praise you. I praise you!" Her transformation in the middle of the bridge was astonishing. I stopped crying and just stared at her. She became instantly composed, and so did I. The presence of the Lord filled the car. His peace was palpable.

When we reached Pastor Becton's home, he met us at the door with a loving embrace. He drove us to the funeral home and instructed us to pick out the finest casket. The churches in the area spared no expense paying for his funeral and transporting the body by plane to New Jersey. They also sent a couple and a young man to follow us home, where they stayed with us for two weeks.

Thirty-eight years later, when I was in the hospital in a battle for my life and the panic was rising, my mind's eye sent me back to that bridge in Westlake, Louisiana. I remembered my mother praising God in the midst of the inexplicable. Out of my mouth I began to do the same thing. I began to sing for all I was worth. I began to praise God for His sovereign control over my life. I didn't care who heard me or what they thought about it. I praised my way out of danger.

My daughter's call that night reminded me that I had been walking the tightrope of my life praising God. By His power, I had made it safely to the other side of so many trials, just as my father and mother had done. Each challenge in the face of the roar of the waves and the foggy mist was a chance for God to show up in all His magnificence.

The same God who showed up for me when I was in danger the year before was still walking every step of the way with me in the second half of 2012. He is the same yesterday, today, and forever (Hebrews 13:8). He will be faithful to complete the good work He has begun in me (Phillipians 1:6). That did not include dropping me now. I knew that the timing of both that man's walk across Niagara Falls and my daughter's phone call to me was providential. God was letting me know that He is the Lord of the wind and the waves and He is in control of my life. I need to keep my eyes fixed on my purpose and look straight ahead. The Holy Spirit is balancing me as I hold tightly to Him and place one foot in front of the other. God has promised, *"Your castles and strongholds shall have bars of iron and bronze, and as your day, so shall your strength be"* (Deuteronomy 33:25).

The peace of God once again began to flood my spirit. I began to thank God for what He had done before and what was still to come. Whatever it was, He was LARGE and IN CHARGE. No weapon formed against me was going to prosper (Isaiah 54:17)! That night, I began to praise God for my job at the cosmetic counter. I began to thank Him that there are no accidents with Him, only incidents.

"Thank God in everything, for this is the will of God for you in Christ Jesus" (1 Thessalonians 5:18). The Bible does not say to be thankful for everything. It says to be thankful in everything. I began to understand that when you begin to be thankful regardless of your circumstances, God shows up!

I had no idea how much He was going to show up in the cosmetics department. In the months that followed, I gave many makeup lessons. More importantly, God led me back to a place I would never have wanted to go, to allow me to take some makeup lessons with Him, and to give me a personal makeover. It was all a part of His plan. He was conforming me more and more to His image by showing me that there is no person, trial or tribulation, no mistake or poor choice in my past that is beyond His ability to redeem.

Makeup Lesson 1: Introduction

I have written this book with four elements. The first is my spiritual journey represented by the stories in each of the chapters that follow. My prayer is that you will find them helpful in your own spiritual journey. Each story ends with a prayer that I have written in a way that you can make each prayer your own for the people and the challenges in your life. At the end of the chapters is a page that lists all the Bible references in this book. I hope this is helpful for individuals and groups who want to include this book in their own Bible study.

Second, each chapter contains a panel that looks like this. Each panel is a makeup lesson, or tip. I have written these lessons in the sequence I would use with a new customer who sits in my chair for a makeover. My purpose in these is not to be the final authority on each subject, but rather to give you enough information that you have confidence and comfort when you sit down with a professional makeup consultant for your own makeover. I understand that not every woman may be able to afford all the products from a prestige cosmetics line to follow every lesson. Therefore, each lesson has a dollar symbol which indicates the relative level of expense you could expect to pay for such products. If you have a tight budget, I recommend you focus on the following lessons: 1, 3, 5, 7, 11, 13-18. Do what you can; add more as your budget allows. Also, give your makeup consultant your contact information so that she can contact you in order to take advantage of seasonal gift promotions from your favorite product line and save money.

Third, after the last chapter I have included a section for you to create your own scrapbook, or journal, just as I describe in Lesson 9. Fill this space with your own creativity. For example, use this space to write your own stories and prayers. Include pictures or drawings of the people and situations for which you are praying to God for victory or protection. Include pictures of yourself before and after your own makeover. Consider doing this with other friends, family, or coworkers who are also reading this book, and watch what God does in your life.

Finally, the end of the book has a series of blank makeup palettes for the eyes, cheeks, lips, and nails. You can bring this book with you when you go for a makeup consultation. Use these palettes to explore and record up to four new makeup looks for yourself and the products used in each.

Lesson #2

The Smallest Details

My first lesson was about practicing my new attitude of gratitude for my job at the cosmetics counter. In obedience to my revelation that God had a sovereign purpose for my life, I developed the habit of praying in the car on the way to work and singing praise songs to Him. My prayer commute helped me to feel more peaceful, focused, and ready to receive whatever opportunity God would bring me that day.

> *"God, I praise You. Thank You for this day, and thank You for my job that gives me the ability to pay my bills. Use me to serve Your purpose."*

I confess that I sometimes felt disappointed when I went to work because, as the new sales consultant in the bay, I had the worst hours for sales on the worst days. The other three women in the bay had the best hours on the best days and made the most money. The worst hours for sales were either early in the morning or late at night when customer traffic was the lightest.

So on this particular morning, instead of letting this disappointment govern my attitude, I kept repeating my prayer silently to myself as I started my shift early that day. There were only two consultants on staff at the time in the entire cosmetics department. I was keeping myself occupied by cleaning the counters and stocking the drawers. Suddenly, this woman came in looking very tense and harried. As we were trained to do, I walked over to her and politely asked, "What can I help you find today, ma'am?"

"Nothing, thank you," she said abruptly. She continued walking all over the department, arbitrarily sampling this and that. She seemed to be stuck in front of the blush display, shaking her head with apparent frustration.

After watching her become more irritated, I approached her again and said, "Ma'am, it seems as though you're struggling to make a choice. Is there any way I can help you?"

She looked up at me, shook her head, and said, "You know, I am just beyond caring."

"Oh!" I said as I reached out and touched her arm. "Don't say that."

Her response was somewhat rambling and unfocused. "Oh, I don't know what I'm doing here. Actually, I'm here today because my sister says that I look too pale, like death warmed over… and I'm trying to choose a blush… and I can't decide if I want this color or that color." One blush was a pink, and the other was a peach.

Then she looked at me and said, "You know, this all seems so silly because I am going to be spending the rest of the day trying to find a nursing home that will care for my forty-six year old daughter who is in a coma and will never wake up. Right about now, I can't seem to make up my mind about something as insignificant as a blush." At that moment, she burst into tears.

I was stunned at first, but I quickly realized that I might be a divine appointment for this woman. Because I am a nurturer, I instinctively reached out to hold her, and I said, "You know, ma'am, you're in a horrible place. I'm a Christian. Would you let me pray for you?"

"Oh, yes. I'm a Christian, too. I have a lot of people praying for me, but today just seems so… I just feel overwhelmed. I can't seem to make any decisions. I don't know where to go or what to do."

So I said to her, "Well, first things first. I think you should buy that blush." I pointed to the peach blush because I believed it would be more attractive on her than the pink. "Yes, you should definitely purchase that peach blush."

I continued, "Now that we have the blush figured out, I just want to ask you a question. My schedule is different every week. Could it be possible that you came to this store, at this time, for a reason? And could it be possible that God knew that I would be here to help you pick out a blush. If God cared that much about giving you assistance with something you consider so insignificant, then how much more will He be there for you to help you choose something where your daughter is concerned?"

She stopped crying and just stood there staring at me with an astonished look on her face. I was able to comfort her. "God cares about everything in your life, down to what you think is the most insignificant. If you are having trouble making choices, He will make sure that someone is there to help you with your daughter."

She turned to the mirror to try on the blush. I found myself praying for her silently.

> *"Father, God, please help this precious woman. I know how it feels when you think you have come to the end of your rope. Life can be so full of insurmountable challenges. You will have to provide the way around, over, or through. Jesus, please be the way-maker for Your daughter who is desperate for You to come with answers."*

I was intimidated by my surroundings. My heart was crying out for her as I was waiting on her. I was so startled by the interaction, that it was even taking place. She was a client. I was supposed to be serving her needs as a makeup consultant, not her spiritual advisor. When I finished praying, I could tell that the peace of God had just come over her. She was smiling as she made her purchase and walked out of the department.

This was a turning point for me. I was seeing confirmation of my belief that God had placed me here in the cosmetics bay on purpose. For the first time, I felt God saying to me in my spirit, "I have given you a great project to do, 'In Search of Steel Magnolias'. I am well aware of what I have equipped you to do and the dreams I have placed within you. I know the ultimate purpose for your life, and what I want to do through you. What if, however, I needed you to take a time out to be in the cosmetics department when a certain lady would come in completely frightened and totally desperate? What if I needed you to show her that I care about the color blush she wears, so that she would know that I loved her enough to care about the treasure of her heart, her daughter? Would that be okay with you?"

I was also dealing with the fact that I was surprised by the incident. I felt convicted by the Holy Spirit that I did not offer to pray for her out loud, right there. Frankly, this had never happened to me before. I believed that I had been so beaten down, that I yielded to unseen social pressures not to pray publically. What if someone overheard me? Would it cost me my job? So I prayed silently.

God's purpose for me is not just wrapped up in that great big thing that I call my destiny or my ultimate purpose. Every day that I get up, every day that I breathe, I am living the purpose of God. I am about Kingdom business, and it is up to God how He chooses to use me. Ministry is not something that I just do; it can be who I am. When I show up, the Kingdom of God shows up. The purpose of God is revealed whenever I engage with anyone. I never know when God is going to place a demand on me.

I gave my heart to Christ in one of my father's revival meetings when I was five years old, and I was baptized when I was seven. I am now fifty-five years old. Nothing in my life ever prepared me for the experiences I would have in the next year where God would use me this way at the makeup counter. I started thinking to myself, "Why is this happening now?" I realized that it was probably always happening. I just wasn't aware of it. I wasn't getting up every morning when my feet hit the floor expecting that today I was going to have a divine appointment with somebody that needed the Jesus within me. His arms to hug them. His words to encourage them. His feet to take them something, or go somewhere with them. The purpose of God was living and breathing in me moment by moment.

Now that I was alert and open to this way of thinking, I was starting to anticipate these opportunities. I never knew what would happen. I certainly didn't create this moment with the woman trying to choose a blush, nor any of the other moments that follow in this book. I did not initiate any of these experiences. I just went to work, took care of my business, and they happened. I was so grateful that they did, and still do.

I encourage you to embark on an experiment with me. Take the next thirty days and pray the following prayer each day. After that, go about your business. Be sensitive to the divine appointments of the Holy Spirit. I believe you will have multiple chances to bring the Kingdom of God to the earth in a unique and powerful way. When the time comes, don't be afraid. When you open your mouth to speak, He will fill it with what He wants you to say. It is a divine partnership. You will never be the same again.

Abba Father, thank You so much for the chance to be a source of encouragement to someone today. I am an alert and willing vessel for You. Please inhabit me by the power of the Holy Spirit. I yield every part of me for Your Kingdom purpose. By Your grace, I refuse to be intimidated by my surroundings. Give me wisdom and sensitivity as to what I should say or do. My purpose is not to preach or be obnoxious and overly zealous in my approach. Help me to go about my business waiting for You to give me divine appointments. When I see them, help me to pray quietly for Your direction as to how You want to use me at that moment.

Nothing in my life is by chance. You are the sovereign of the universe. You will direct me to accomplish Your purpose in the earth. I am in this job by divine order. I am an ambassador from a Heavenly Kingdom to this earth. Let Your light shine inside of me wherever I am. Make Yourself known to me this day. When opportunities present themselves, help me not to shrink back in fear of anyone for any reason. You and I are going to walk out this life of mine together. When I see You face to face, I want to hear You say, "Well done, My good and faithful servant!" It is Your smile of approval I seek. It is Your love that I live for and Your endorsement that matters. You are my Father, and I am Your child. I love You, and I am thankful that You love me.

In Jesus' name and for His sake, so be it!

Makeup Lesson 2: Makeup and Skincare Consultation

($0) If you were going to trust someone to remodel your house, you would more than likely do some research. The end product will be the result of the talent, skill, knowledge and professionalism of your contractor. If you go to see a doctor to trust him with your body and address specific concerns, then you will have researched him or her and gotten a reference from someone you trust. If there is a costly diagnosis or remodeling plan, you will more than likely have gotten two or three other bids or medical opinions.

An annual skin care consultation should be as much of a priority as a biannual dental cleaning or an annual physical exam. You have to separate skin care that, in my opinion, is not an option, and makeup, which is an optional application and expense. You can tell so much about what is going on inside a person by the look and texture of their skin. Sometimes, skin issues raise a red flag that tells you something is wrong inside your body.

Shop for a consultant the same way you would a doctor, a dentist, or anyone else that I consider has valuable information at a price. There are many reputable product lines in the cosmetic industry which have been around for a century. The professionals who work for them are trained several times a year by account executives with the newest information regarding the science of skin care. It does not cost anything to make an appointment and talk to them. Develop a rapport with them. Do they listen to you? Are they solution-oriented? If they are talking more than listening and overwhelming you with products you did not request, then you are in the wrong place. It is your money that you're spending, and you deserve to be heard and to have your needs met. This will only truly happen to the extent that you trust your consultant about your true concerns, allow them access to you, and have realistic expectations about products results. You want someone who will tell you the truth. You want someone who is informed and someone who will understand your financial limitations. Ask women whom you admire about the consultants they see. Then search for yourself. What works for them might not work for you.

Lesson #3

Panic is Your Enemy

Three days later I was back at work. It was 9:30 at night. Once again, I was one of only two consultants in the cosmetics department. All the customers had gone home. My feet hurt. The pain was undeniable when I was bored with nothing to do. When I was busy, it was easy to ignore the painful blisters from my new shoes. Instead, I was counting the minutes until the clock struck ten and I could go home. My thoughts would play over and over in my mind like a broken record. What am I doing here? How do I reinvent my life yet again? How long do I stay here? Again, I would find myself quietly singing praise choruses and talking to God about this messed up tapestry of my life. It felt as though I was looking on the backside of an embroidery piece with lots of loose threads. I could see the basic outline, but it was not an image that a person would want to display proudly. I would find myself pouring my heart out to God desperately seeking His guidance and answers to my questions. What were the next threads to be sown into my life?

I was about to close the register when an attractive Asian woman entered my bay. I asked her, "May I help you?"

She curtly said, "No." She bounced from display to display as she tried on lipsticks, eyeliners, blushes, and just about everything else. She was getting increasingly agitated, but she did not want any assistance. I stood by quietly trying not to seem pushy.

Finally, I approached her and said, "Miss, we'll be closing in fifteen minutes. It seems you are having trouble choosing. I'm glad to help if I can."

She stood at the counter, looked at me, hung her head, covered her face, and broke down sobbing. My maternal instincts kicked in. I grabbed her hand and started to console her as best I could. She looked up with panic in her eyes. Very quietly, through clenched teeth, she said, "You don't understand. I cannot fail. I am going back to university and I cannot fail. I am buying these cosmetics because I start class tomorrow, and I want to look my best. I cannot fail. I can't seem to choose what will look best on me."

She looked completely terrified. So I asked her, "May I make a suggestion?" I looked at her choices and told her which products I felt would suit her best.

Then I asked her, "Do you really want these items? You are not going to fix your problems buying makeup costing hundreds of dollars. You might regret it in the morning and come back to return it."

She stopped her crying, thought for a moment, and said, "No. No, I need these things. I want to look my best."

I said, "Okay, if you're sure, then I recommend these."

Then I added, "May I offer you something to consider? You seem to be about the same age as my daughter." She smiled sweetly through her tears and nodded yes.

I continued, "Your panic is your enemy, not the task. You cannot think emotionally and rationally at the same time. There was a time of great fear in my life. Circumstances justified the emotional reaction. I understand all too well how hard it is to concentrate when you are in an upsetting situation and have to tackle a challenge or an obstacle. Do you go to church?"

She said, "I have recently moved to Dallas. I had been trying to find a church, but I couldn't decide on one. Now life has become too busy, and I've stopped pursuing it."

"I understand. I suggest that, for the time being at least, you try to find a quiet place for fifteen minutes a day and just be still. Sometimes you just need to breathe."

I paused briefly, and then said, "When I feel confused, I pray. I give my problems to God and ask Him to help me find solutions. Would you mind if I prayed for you right now?" I realized that God was giving me a makeup lesson not to be intimidated by my environment. I made the choice with this woman not to care what anyone thought, but to be obedient and responsive to His prompting. She was someone's daughter, and to myself I silently prayed that if my children were ever out there in need of help or consolation, then God would send them a believer who would not be afraid to pray for them if they needed prayer.

She said excitedly, "Oh, would you?" I grabbed both of her hands in mine and I prayed:

> *"Father, give this precious young woman Your peace that passes understanding. Let it flood every part of her being. I ask that she would be filled with the mind of Christ and that He would give her the ability to retain knowledge in all her subjects. In Jesus' name, I pray. Amen."*

It was a simple prayer. When I finished, she started to cross herself and then stopped because she remembered that we were standing in the department store. I guessed she was Catholic. We both laughed as I noticed her looking nervously to her left and right, but there wasn't a soul around.

I finished her transaction exactly at ten p.m. I hugged her and told her where my church was if she would like to visit. I told her that she could call my church hotline at any time to leave a prayer request, and she would receive prayer regularly. Her whole attitude and demeanor was completely different when she left, as though the weight of the world had been lifted from her shoulders.

I stood there quietly for a moment in complete awe. God was so real to me. He was with the two of us as we spoke. I felt His presence. I knew that once again He had orchestrated my schedule that week. He did not want me there in the daytime when the store would have been busy. God needed me at the end of the day, for this precious young woman, when there would be nobody around, and she would not be embarrassed. I belonged to Him, and He had an appointment with a terrified little girl in a grown up body. This was Kingdom purpose flowing through me! When my shift was over, I walked to my car in the empty parking lot while the Fourth of July was going on in my heart.

Even with my new attitude and practice of praying on my way to work, I still had no idea that many more divine encounters would be coming. I sensed that I was on assignment. The Lord needed me here and now. He was going to do a work in me and through me at the same time. God was using me to give makeup lessons to His daughters while He was doing a makeover on me. Wow! What an awesome God!

Abba Father, thank You for using me! Jesus died to give me salvation and purpose in this life. Lord, true success is being in the center of Your will for my life. There is nothing as thrilling in the whole world as knowing that I am where You want me to be. I am grateful that no matter how far off course I think I may be, You will still use me for Your glory.

Teach me how to see my life through Your eyes. Help me to understand that it is not necessary for me to fear anything. Your perfect love casts out all fear. Because of You, I can walk freely and with no condemnation, knowing that You are high and lifted above the whole earth and all the circumstances in my life.

I want to hear Your voice clearly. I bind myself to the mind of Christ. His thoughts, will and purpose become mine when I yield myself completely to Him. I can face what I need to face and learn what I need to know, because Your Holy Spirit will assist me in all my endeavors. I thank You for peace. I refuse to panic about any situation, because You have already been in my future. You will be a lamp unto my feet and a light unto my path. You said so, and that is all I need to know. That is why today is going to be a great day, because whatever happens, we will face it together.

I love You!

In Jesus' name. So be it!

Makeup Lesson 3: Plastic Surgery

($$$$$) Plastic surgery can be a blessing to women who have been disfigured by any number of causes. In such cases, it is not a radical solution, but a tool that can give women a new lease on life and help them regain their self-esteem. I am grateful they have this option. Some things can only be corrected by surgery.

I am extremely concerned, however, about the demand for elective plastic surgery in our culture. Today, many women face the pressure to be what they are not in order to feel wanted and desired. No amount of cream can fix certain physical issues related to age and lifestyle. We will age. It is a fact. If surgery can assist with self-esteem when diet and exercise do not work, then it is about personal choice. I am concerned about the motivation for the decision to have plastic surgery. God loves us. Our self-worth should be anchored in Him. Each woman should pray about it, make a decision with input from the Holy Spirit, and be very careful. If a woman makes this choice to earn someone's love, in spite of potential clear risks to your health, it is not worth it. At some point in time, we have to be content with "Whose" we are. Some people may walk away if you are not perfect enough, so let them go!

A couple of anecdotes: First, there was a middle-aged woman who had such low self-esteem. She belonged to several dating websites but complained that she could not get a man interested in her. One man showed up for a date, took one look at her and said, "You look older than your picture." He promptly turned around, got in his car, and drove away. Experiences like this motivated her to pay $16,000 for a facelift. That surgery resulted in blood clots so severe that she could not get out of bed for months, and had to be cared for by her eighty year old mother. There is a test that you can take which will alert you to whether or not you are prone to blood clots. She did not know about this test. She almost lost her life.

Second, another woman had radical liposuction from her neck to her knees. After surgery, her husband had to bathe her and wrap her body in bandages. It took her six months to recover fully. She never had any intention of changing her lifestyle or eating habits. She eventually gained all the weight back and more. Plastic surgery is a decision which should be entered into after great thought and research, not out of desperation.

Lesson #4

Serve without Judging

When you apply to work for a major department store and the store hires you, the Human Resources department gives you a series of questionnaires you have to answer regarding your attitudes toward protected classes and minorities in our society. In addition, you participate in training to reinforce the company objective of fair and equal treatment of all customers. The company wants to make sure that you are not going to manifest prejudice or bigotry toward anyone.

On a typical afternoon during the week, I was working at my bay when two gentlemen came in, one older, the other younger. The older man asked me to do a complete makeover on the younger man, including skin care and a full makeover with mascara, lipstick, and blush. I realized that, as a professional in that store, I was not allowed to refuse service to anyone, or to make any client feel uncomfortable. Frankly, it never occurred to me that a man would come in and want me to make him up as a woman. I was so completely startled by this situation. I… I really… I knew I had to do my best as a professional not to let anything register on my face, even though I had strong feelings. Internally, I was wrestling with my own sense of awkwardness.

At the same time, I suspected that this could be a setup to see how I would handle this situation. Was the company testing me because something like this could happen in the future? Was the company assessing my professionalism? I was not sure if this was real, but I proceeded instinctively to treat this young man as any other client.

I began by analyzing his skin. He seemed to me to be extremely shy and nervous. Makeovers in our department store are generally free, but when someone asks for a makeover there is an implied understanding that the consultant will present each one of the products to the client. The goal is to get clients to buy one or two of the products presented. Even if clients don't buy anything immediately, they should know what they like when making a future purchase.

I seated the young man, and then started by applying a cleanser. As I put my hands all over his face, I noticed that he reacted like a scared rabbit. He would flinch slightly each time my feminine hands would touch his masculine face to add more cleanser, or apply the makeup. Even though I also felt uncomfortable, I continued my routine.

At some point during the process, my heart went out to him. I thought to myself that it must be very hard to be caught between two worlds. As I was going through my product presentation, he was clearly becoming more uncomfortable. He did not "own" the makeover experience. I began to feel compassion for this man. I made up my mind, with conviction this time, that I was a professional and I was going to treat him as I would any other female client.

At this moment, I recognized that functioning in agape love, which is God's kind of love, requires a decision. Love is an action verb accompanied by feelings. I found myself wondering, "Is this how God responds when He watches my behavior and disagrees with me, but still extends His love and compassion toward me?" I am sure that Jesus did not "feel" like going to the cross for mankind considering that He knew what is in the hearts of men. When He begged God in the Garden of Gethsemane to "let this cup pass from Him", He knew that choosing to love His persecutors would have mortal consequences. Agape love does not depend on the other person, their actions, appearance, or beliefs. If Jesus could lay down His life for His persecutors, then shouldn't I who claim to follow Him be able to serve those who are different and do it willingly? *"Therefore be imitators of God, as well-beloved children. And walk in love, as Christ loved us and gave Himself up for us, a slain offering and sacrifice to God for you, so that it became a sweet fragrance"* (Ephesians 5:1-2). I always find that when I make the choice to love what is hard for me to love, the grace of God begins to flow through me, and my feelings come into alignment.

Jesus said, *"By this shall all men know that you are My disciples, if you love one another"* (John 13:35). This is a defining statement. Love is supposed to be our ID badge as Christians. Do we measure ourselves as Christians by how well we speak "Christianese", or by our church attendance, or by which "flavor" of Jesus we are? Or do we measure ourselves by the way we love? Christ came to save the world, not condemn it. After all, He ate dinner with Zaccheus, the tax collector, ministered to the Samaritan woman at the well, and healed the lepers. He disregarded the religious and cultural prejudices of His time. Who, therefore, are we to condemn anyone? Can we at least be polite?

I found that the more that I touched this young man, and the more I worked on him and treated him as a person with respect, kindness, and professionalism, the less awkward I began to feel. I used this opportunity to express grace and kindness toward someone to whom many in our world might not be so kind. When I was finished, they purchased some items. I thanked them, and they left the department.

A few minutes later the older gentleman came back and said, "I want to thank you very much for being so respectful. This young man is in the process of preparing for the surgery that will be necessary to complete his gender reassignment."

"You're welcome," I replied. "I'm just doing my job."

"Well, thank you very, very much." And he walked away. As I watched him leave, I began to understand that I move in this world among people who may challenge my beliefs on many levels. Still, every person who crosses my path is someone for whom Jesus also died. Even if no one else existed on the planet, God would have sent Jesus to die for that young man.

What should my response be in these situations? Through this experience, I determined that God was showing me that there would always be opportunities for me to choose to show agape love to someone who was vastly different from me. As long as I made the choice to be obedient, then the love of God would meet me in that moment and flow through me. I decided to withhold my judgment and to express the love of God by serving him. It was not my responsibility to question his motives or preach to him about his lifestyle. It was my job to serve him without judging or passing sentence.

I continue to intercede for this young man, believing that God will find Him.

> *"Father, speak to the heart of this young man, somehow, someway. Just like me, I know that You created him in Your image and You do not make mistakes. He is precious in Your sight. Lord, Your Word teaches me that You are not the author of confusion. I may be confused at times, but You are not. You know exactly why You have created me. I know that You considered him, too, when You sent Your Son Jesus to die on the cross and bring salvation to all mankind."*

When God reveals to us as individuals how willing He was to send His Son as a sacrifice for our sins, it ends the crisis of confusion. Unfortunately, many people live their lives afraid of God believing they will receive only condemnation if they admit their confusion or take their sins to Him. God may have a very bad public relations problem. His children, His representatives on earth have not always done an exemplary job of communicating His loving heart, and the lengths He would go to win a lost world that so desperately needs Him.

I do not feel the need to talk anybody into Jesus theologically. I would just like to introduce them to a Savior who would go to hell and back for them, and did! My daddy used to say, "If you can talk somebody into Jesus, then someone else can come along and talk that person right out of Him." When a person comes to know and love Jesus as I do, He will make whatever changes in that person that He deems best. One thing is for sure - I am counting on Jesus to do the same for me.

When I fully comprehend that I am the recipient of God's love, which is beyond all measure, I can love myself and others. Also, the pressure to reinvent myself in order to earn acceptance from others is gone. I understand what it means to be accepted by the Beloved. I can breathe. God has accepted me. Jesus loves me just as I am and where I am, but He never leaves me there. He always calls me to come up higher.

God is the one who changes us from glory to glory. That is the job of the Holy Spirit. I am not Holy Spirit Junior. If God uses me to speak a word of correction to someone, then I should speak the truth in love. Sometimes we may not speak the truth because we are afraid of the consequences. Other times we do not speak the truth in love, and it becomes our sword that we use to cut people. Both ways are ineffective. You can be "right" all day long and leave some poor soul broken and bleeding all over the place with the truth. The Truth is not something to be discovered. The Truth is Jesus, who revealed, "I am the Way and the Truth and the Life" (John 14:6). When you know the Truth, He will lead you into all truth, which is the Word of God. This combination will set you free, and never leave you shattered.

I maintain that almost every behavioral issue or conflict we may have in our lives that God would want to change is a result of a relationship crisis. First, we do not really know the nature of God. "*...You are a God ready to pardon, gracious and merciful, slow to anger, and of great steadfast love*" (Nehemiah 9:17).

Second, we do not know our relationship to Him. "*For the Spirit which you have now received is not a spirit of slavery to put you once more in bondage to fear, but you have received the Spirit producing sonship in which we cry, Abba! Father! The Spirit Himself thus testifies together with our own spirit, assuring us that we are children of God. And if we are His children, then we are His heirs also: heirs of God and fellow heirs with Christ*" (Romans 8:15-17).

Finally, we do not know all we can do through Him. "*... we are more than conquerors and gain a surpassing victory through Him Who loved us*" (Romans 8:37).

If we would just run to God instead of running away from Him, we would find that His love is deep enough to handle our secret sins, and His grace is sufficient to cover and cleanse us from anything that shames us.

The bottom line is this: God is God, and we are not. As His children, we are His spokesmen on the earth. We will stand before Him to answer one day for our own lives, as well as for the voice we have been on His behalf.

Abba Father, I want to walk on this earth as an instrument of Your mercy and grace. Help me to realize how gracious You have been to me when You have dealt with my sins and shortcomings. You have said that we all have sinned and fall short of Your glory. All means ALL. That includes me. Deal with my pride and arrogance. Help me to see people as You see them. Teach me the difference between discipline and punishment. You punished Jesus for my sins. He took them upon Himself. He paid the price. Help me now to understand that you administer loving discipline for the purpose of correcting my course. There is a difference. You will have well-behaved children. Your interest is that I become all that You created me to be.

Please help me to express accurately Your love to the world that so desperately needs You. Give me a sense of conviction when I have failed to do this appropriately and have caused people emotional and spiritual harm. Speak through me.

In Jesus' name, so be it!

Makeup Lesson 4: Skin Care

($) Proper skin care is not a vanity issue. It is a health issue. If you give priority to taking care of your skin, you will look younger for longer. Experts tell us that eighty-five percent of all aging to the skin is not a reflection of your chronological age. It is largely due to your genetics, personal lifestyle and environmental hazards. Pollution, free radicals, exposure to the sun and other elements, food, and cigarette smoke all play a part in the aging process.

Invest in a skin care system that is targeted specifically to your skin type and concerns. Your personal skin care system should consist of the following steps: a cleanser, toner, serum, moisturizer and eye serum followed by eye cream. The skin on your body is like construction paper. The skin on your face is comparable to computer paper, while the skin around your eyes is like tissue paper. Thus, the formulations are different in each product. More is not better. Using a large amount of a good thing will not cause you to reap a better result. It is wasteful and can even be counterproductive.

Next, use an exfoliating cleanser twice per week. There is a difference in the beads in the prestige lines vs. some less expensive products. The prestige lines have perfectly manufactured beads which don't tear the skin, as opposed to fragments that tear. Use a clay masque once per week, or perhaps less if your skin tends to be dry.

Do not neglect the rest of your body, neck, or chest area, which is also called your décolleté. We frequently pay attention to our faces, but neglect the neckline, the chest area and the arms and elbows. There are wonderful exfoliating cleansers for the body, to be followed by rich body creams which will nourish your skin.

The prestige lines now carry products that fight cellulite and treatments for stretch marks. Do not confuse these topical treatments with plastic surgery. There is no miracle in a bottle. There is, however, the ability to expect some significant transformation. You perceive the entire world through your skin. It is imperative that you pay attention to it. Look at your whole body at least once a month. Watch for any changes that might cause concern.

Lesson #5

God Knows Your Needs

As a new, part-time consultant, I needed training in the product line for the brand I was representing. As the rookie on the team with no customer base, management scheduled me for the odd work shifts, such as Sunday morning. I understood why they did this. We sell a prestigious product. One cream could cost as much as $250. Some people are inclined to say things such as, "You spent how much on that?" Or, "It's all about the brand name!" Does brand determine price? Of course, there is a factor in the pricing that is due to the branding behind the product. On the other hand, I was impressed by how much research and development goes into the development of high-end cosmetics. There is a tremendous science behind all the products. I had to learn a lot of technical terms and information during my training. A good makeup consultant uses her knowledge to match the product to a client's specific concern.

Even though I understood I was in training, it was still a challenge to feel motivated going to work expecting not to make many sales. In addition to my modest hourly wage, part of my compensation was based on commission. My problem was that I had been out of work. I needed to make some money quickly. Without the opportunity to make decent sales, my part-time wages were not going to meet my immediate needs.

I kept reminding myself of the conscious decision I made to get part-time work that would give me the flexibility to pursue my passion project, "In Search of Steel Magnolias". Despite this, from time to time I would still hear the little devil and angel on my shoulders going back and forth:

[Devil] "Why is she here? She isn't going to make any money. She should quit!"
[Angel] "She knows why she's here. Clearly God is using her. God has put her here. She knows that."
[Me] "Hush!"

One Sunday, my manager scheduled me to start at 10:30 am and finish at 1:30. Now this is Dallas, the heart of the Bible belt. On a Sunday morning, hardly anyone is shopping at the mall.

People start coming in to shop after church around one or two o'clock. And frankly, God help you if the Cowboys are playing football. It is relatively easy to predict when business is going to be slow.

When I got to my bay, I looked at the scheduled for that day. I had the morning shift. Another consultant would come in to take my place to work the busier afternoon shift. The goal for the day was $500 each, or $1,000 combined. I looked at that goal and thought, *This is ridiculous! I'm going to be standing here. There's not a soul that's going to be coming in here until it's time for me to leave.*

Well, I was there barely 40 minutes when a woman dressed in workout clothes came up to me. "Good morning!"

I approached her and replied, "Good morning, ma'am. How may I help you?" My expectations were still low. It was 11:30 and there was no one else in the store.

"I'm in a hurry, but I need to replace a few items." Before I knew it, she started to walk around the counter and chirped, "I'll have this, and this, and this, and this, and this…"

I couldn't believe it! This woman bought $450 worth of product from me. With one sale, I was only $50 shy of my goal. Suddenly, one after another, people starting coming up to me to purchase cosmetics. By the time I left at 1:30, just two hours later, my sales had totaled $960 - just $40 less than the combined goal for the day. The consultant coming to relieve me took one look at the sales for the day and just shook her head. She couldn't believe it. I couldn't believe it! I walked out of the store and started laughing because I heard the Lord say to me, "You go where I tell you to go. You do what I tell you to do. Your needs are My business. You take care of My business, and I'll take care of your business."

That's the way He launched me in my part-time job. I couldn't get over what had happened. So, I started praising God. Now, I don't sell $1,000 worth of cosmetics every time I go to work, but I will tell you that over the last year God has creatively helped me meet my needs. For example, I was concerned about my car, which I had purchased in 2004. The car had been reliable, but by the end of 2012, it had close to 100,000 miles. I had less and less confidence in my car continuing to operate without being surprised by a major repair bill. I had started working in June and that next January I got a postcard from a local dealer offering me a good trade-in value on my car in exchange for buying a new one of the same model with nothing else down. Because I had a job, I was able to do exactly that.

Additionally, MDS employees received product discounts, which enabled me to update my wardrobe inexpensively. I would multiply the savings by waiting for items I wanted to go on sale. This was significant to me because I had recently lost about 40 lbs and desperately needed some new clothes. Because I worked at the cosmetics counter, not only did I take advantage of the gift seasons, I also got product gratis from each training session I attended. This would have totaled hundreds of dollars for very expensive cosmetics.

All this was building me up. I had reliable transportation again. I also had a new wardrobe, and I looked better than I had looked in years. I had skin care, cosmetics and fragrances that I would never have been able to afford otherwise. God was restoring me. I was experiencing the spiritual law of reaping and sowing (Galatians 6:7-9). I was sowing encouragement into all these women, praising God and thanking Him for being there, even though I was not earning a lot of money. As a result, I was reaping the various ways God provided to encourage me and bless me financially.

I saw the cycle of give and take. I saw the flow between God and me. My choice: praise and obedience. Do what I am told to do. Do it praising Him with a sweet spirit. Then watch God take care of my business as I take care of His business. I discovered that it is impossible to out-give God.

In the spirit realm, when you plant or sow something, the harvest is usually not immediate. Yes, God can bless you with significant results quickly, particularly when you are just starting your walk with Him, and you are learning how to give so that it is given unto you. *"Give and gifts will be given to you; good measure, pressed down, shaken together, and running over, will they pour into the bosom of your robe. For with the measure you deal out, it will be measured back to you"* (Luke 6:38).

Otherwise, it is like any time you plant something in the ground. You don't plant and then go out the next morning to see a crop ready to harvest. First, the seed has to die. In this case, death to me meant my pride. I had been a producer, travelling back and forth across the country filming events. Here I was working retail again where I had been thirteen years before as a struggling, single mother. I had to be willing to lay those painful memories at the feet of Jesus and say, "Lord, if I must do this to pay my bills while You establish that which I believe You have called me to do, then I'm going to die to my pride. I am going to abandon my agenda and submit to Yours. I'm going to be here with a good attitude and a sweet spirit."

A seed dies first, then it grows down. I must learn to build a strong foundation of obedience. I will be here as long as God has me here; as long as He wants me here. I trust Him that He is going to make the difference, and make up the difference. This is growing down to create my root system.

After a period of time when the seed has grown down, it starts to grow up. Growing up in Christ means I have mastered the ability to trust and obey. There is an old hymn:

"Trust and obey,
For there is no other way
To be happy in Jesus."

Trust and obey. Every day I go to work – I TRUST: You are going to meet my needs. Okay – I OBEY. Trust. Obey. I submit to the process in order to mature in Christ.

The seed becomes a plant and begins to grow out. In my life, I suddenly began to see fruit. All my dreams and desires began to take shape (Matthew 6:33). I had opportunities to develop my passion project, "In Search of Steel Magnolias". I was also able to fly to New Jersey to participate in a special event. I was growing out. My sphere of influence was widening. People at work were coming to me asking me to pray for them. Then my Bible study group asked me to prepare and present a book review for a book club. This was a new experience for me, but I did it, and everyone gave me overflowing praise. Next came other things that I had not done for years, such as singing and speaking at services. I was growing out after I learned to die to myself, to die to my way of doing things, to stop arguing with God: "What do You mean I'm here? This is not what I'm supposed to be doing. After all, look what I've accomplished. This isn't the plan!" I understand now that sometimes God has taken me back to a place because He wanted to redeem everything that ever happened in my life and turn it for good. He has taken me all the way back to MDS, but the woman who walked into the cosmetics counter at MDS in 2013 was not the same woman who nearly did not walk out of the fine jewelry department thirteen years ago. That woman was a shattered, heartbroken and confused mess. God took me back to a place where he was going to give me some makeup lessons, and do a makeover on me. Then He was going to use me to share that with other people.

God's kingdom is upside-down compared to the kingdoms of this world. God says, *"For My thoughts are not your thoughts, neither are your ways My ways... For as the heavens are higher than the earth so are My ways higher than your ways and My thoughts than your thoughts"* (Isaiah 55:8-9). So how far are His ways from our ways? It's immeasurable. We can never understand the way He thinks by the way we think as human beings functioning in three dimensional space and time. The Word says, *"The natural, non-spiritual man does not accept or welcome or admit into his heart the gifts and teachings and revelations of the Spirit of God, for they are meaningless nonsense to him; and he is incapable of knowing them because they are spiritually discerned and estimated and appreciated"* (1 Corinthians 2:14).

God was the only one that knew the truth about this great job I thought I was going to have. Was it really going to be good for me? If I didn't get it, then was I a failure? God already knew that if I got that job, it might have cost me my marriage or my health. He could see events that were ahead that I did not see because He was looking at my life from His perspective. My human perception of situations was not always accurate. I had limited perspective. He could see my past, present, and future all at the same time. He knew what He was doing. I had to learn to trust Him. The Word of God says, *"Lean on, trust in, and be confident in the Lord with all your heart and mind and do not rely on your own insight or understanding. In all your ways, recognize and acknowledge Him, and He will direct and make straight and plain your paths"* (Proverbs 3:5-6).

If all this was true, then was my return to MDS going backward or forward? To my way of thinking, I would never have considered going back to work in retail as going forward. That was not where I was headed. I had just spent three years working for a production company, traveling around the country, and filming amazing events. Yes, on the surface, it looked as though I was going backward. On the other hand, evaluating everything over the course of a year with all these experiences, what was backward to me was forward to God.

Many measure success by the increase of money, power, and fame. God measures success by the way you love and obey Him, and fulfill His call on your life. Of course, God wants you to prosper and be successful, but He will never measure success the same way you do (3 John 1:2).

So I was constantly receiving confirmation that God had a reason for me to be here at the makeup counter. I was to praise Him, and not blame Him. I was not a failure in His eyes, even though I had failed many times. Growing up in Christ meant I must choose to see things through spiritual eyes with spiritual discernment. I prayed for my children, my husband, and myself all the time: *"God, give me spiritual eyes to see, and ears to hear what Your spirit says."*

I can honestly say that I look forward to going to my part-time job because I am not just selling makeup. I believe that this job is just for a season, and I will move on. While I am here, however, I am excited because I never know what the Lord is going to do next.

Abba Father, You are the source of every good thing. You know exactly what I need financially to survive, and to thrive in this life. You are Jehovah Jireh, the God who provides. Forgive me for looking to people and my job as my source. You are my source. I acknowledge that if I put You and Your Kingdom purpose first in my life, then You promise all other things will be provided.

Show me the path to financial freedom and success. Help me to be in the right place, doing what You have called me to do. I don't want to waste my life where there is no room for me to grow. Help me to know without a shadow of a doubt that I am right where You want me to be. If I am not, please give me the ability to let go and walk away.

There may be times when You give me an assignment that doesn't meet all my needs. Help me to be obedient. Help me also to recognize that I have multiple streams of income placed around me, through which You will provide. Help me to discern my work situation appropriately.

If I need to go back to school or be trained in another field, please give me the confidence to tackle the challenge. Unanticipated obstacles may require me to tap into internal resources that I never realized I had. Even though I may feel intimidated and frightened, You made me, and You know the gifts and talents that You placed within me. Reveal me to myself. I may be unsettled at times and feel as though I am floundering, but You are not.

I am counting on You to give me clear direction. I am counting on Your faithfulness to provide for me. You are completely trustworthy. I commit myself into Your care this day.

In Jesus' name, so be it!

Makeup Lesson 5: Age Prevention and Reversal

($$$) It is a myth that you can stop the aging process, but you can slow it down. You can take care of the one and only body that God has given you. It amazes me how some people take better care of their cars than they do their bodies.

Science is now providing information that can take us a long way in prevention and restoration. There are products that have anti-oxidants previously used in pharmaceutical applications, and are now found in skin care products. These products can reverse damage from the sun on a cellular level.

There are also products that claim to have reproduced human ceramides, creating elasticity and firmness to the skin. Skin cells in the body are like bricks on a house. Ceramides are analogous to mortar. As we age, our ceramides break down the way the mortar may on an aging house.

The biggest way to help delay the aging process is to apply wisdom with your lifestyle and use treatment products that will assist in delaying the inevitable. Drink water. Get plenty of rest. Exercise consistently. Pray daily. Eat the right foods. Laugh a lot! There is power in your thoughts and in the words that come out of your mouth. The body was not meant to inhale smoke. It will age your skin and could give you cancer. Use common sense with activities.

The Internet is a great source of information about ingredients in products to assist with treatment. Have a professional facial at a reputable salon at least quarterly. Various Internet companies offer deals on makeover services, greatly reducing their cost and giving you the opportunity to experience new salons. Taking care of yourself is not selfish. It is necessary and vital to your well-being; more so in times of crisis. Budget time, money, and opportunity to pamper yourself. Typically, women who have given up on the outside of themselves have already given up on the inside of themselves. It is a choice, a reflection of our perceived personal value. Develop a strategy, start with the basics, and then add steps and products as you are able.

Lesson #6

Free Indeed

What to my surprise did the Lord do next? He set up an encounter with a client I never expected on a hot summer day in Dallas, Texas.

Not long after my outstanding Sunday morning sales, I was back at my counter for another shift. I was busy with my head down cleaning and arranging my display cases when I heard a young woman's voice very politely say:

"Excuse me. Could you help me, please? I'm looking for an eye shadow for my sister and me."

Nothing in my mind registered as unusual about this request until I quickly closed my display case and looked up to see a woman completely covered in a black burqa. Now I must have paused for a moment and stuttered slightly as my standard response issued from my mouth, but I don't remember.

"Uh…y..yes, ma'am, I can help you." I tried to compose myself as quickly as possible. "Our eye shadows are right over here." I tried to focus on her eyes, which was all I could see of her face. Her eyes appeared dark brown and penetrating, but sweet, too, as she peered out of the slot in her head covering. Otherwise, she was covered from head to toe in a flowing black gown. In the short time I had been at MDS, I had already waited on several Muslim women shopping in the store. They were, however, always wearing contemporary outfits with very elegant, color-coordinated head coverings. In each case, I could also see that their makeup was meticulously applied.

How in the world was I going to demonstrate cosmetics to this woman? I had this uncomfortable feeling in my whole body. It was so hot outside! I thought to myself that she must be miserable in this outfit. I had seen such women on television, but I had never been this close to a Muslim woman in a burqa, nor talked to one. How awkward it felt to see a woman talking to me but never see her lips move. She started to tell me the shades she wanted by the exact product name. I quickly understood that she was clearly knowledgeable about the product line. Of course, this struck me as odd. Why would a woman in a burqa buy makeup? Did she take off her burqa at home and put on makeup in order to look attractive to her husband, or was buying and wearing makeup an act of defiance to express her individuality in an oppressive environment? It was a mystery to me.

Suddenly, I snapped out of my daze and noticed two precious children near her. They were just as cute as could be – a little boy and his younger sister both dressed in adorable short sets. Apparently nothing about their mother's appearance seemed strange to the children. They were in their own little world playfully talking to each other. The little girl tugged on her mother's dress. The mother looked down at her and said something in Arabic, which seemed to satisfy her enough that she went back to playing with her brother. Then the woman looked at me again and tried to make me feel comfortable by engaging me in dialogue with her accented, but precise English.

"This is new. How beautiful! When did this color come out?"

"About a month ago. It just came out with our new fall line. A lot of the young ladies like the glitter look in these darker shades." By now I noticed that she was not wearing any eye shadow at the moment. "You seem to be familiar with our product line."

"Yes, I am."

Her response helped me to feel more at ease, but I still didn't know what to suggest to her. After all, women typically coordinate their makeup with specific outfits. I let her take the lead in picking out the colors she liked. I was surprised to see that she leaned toward the very bold and dramatic grays, pewters, and blacks. I assumed that she would be interested in the neutral colors, but when I listened to her I understood that she wanted the dark and intense colors.

Normally, I would have volunteered to apply the eye shadow to the client. I didn't dare to go there. I could see the color of her skin from her exposed hand. She had a light, Mediterranean skin tone. I could sense, however, that any touching between us would be uncomfortable for her. Even though my skin is so much fairer than hers, I offered to show the eye shadows to her on the back of my hand.

"You can see here. This darker shade with the lighter purple creates a very dramatic look."

"I like that. I'll take these." She completed her transaction, thanked me graciously, and left with her children. As she walked away, I wondered to myself how a woman grows up to accept dressing like this when, as a child, she probably dressed and played just as her own children do now. No one can see the expression on her face. No one can see her smile or laugh. She looks indistinguishable from any other woman dressed in a black shroud. How does it feel to have to hide your face in public? I found myself thinking she seems to be okay with that, but does she get a choice? I could not imagine myself ever being comfortable living that way.

Later that night, I told my husband about the experience. "I had a client today who was wearing a burqa."

"Really?"

"Yes. She was completely covered in black except for a slit around her eyes. She wanted to buy eye shadow. I know she's Muslim, but I don't know her nationality. Why do some Muslims wear burqas and others don't?"

"I don't know. Let's Google it." My husband is very practical. "Let's see, here. Wikipedia…burqa. Here are some images. You said her head covering had a slot in it, right?"

"Yes."

"That style seems to be called a niqab. A burqa actually has some sort of mesh covering over the eyes. See the difference? You could see her eyes, right?"

"Yes, definitely. Does it say why Muslim women cover themselves?"

"Let's see. It says here..."

"The claimed rationale of the niqab comes from the Qur'an and Hadith. It was known that the wives of the Prophet Muhammad covered themselves around non-mahram (marriageable, unrelated) men. However, the Qur'an explicitly states that the wives of the Prophet are held to a different standard. It is claimed that, under Islam, the niqab is a requirement for all women, since womanhood is mentioned along with the wives of Muhammad in the Qur'anic dictat to cover. The following verse from the Qur'an is cited as support for this:

"'O Prophet! Tell your wives and your daughters, and the believing women, to draw their cloaks (veils) over their bodies. That will be better that they should be known (as respectable woman)' Quran 33:59."

"It also says here that there are different schools of thought about whether or not covering with a niqab is 'obligatory' or 'recommended', depending on the Sunni sect followed. "

"Interesting!"

"I suppose," my husband continued, "that it's similar to different Christian sects."

This surprised me. "What do you mean? I've never seen a Christian woman cover herself like this."

"No. But I know, for example, that years ago Catholic women would cover their head with a scarf or veil when they went to mass. And you know quite well from your own background that, in certain conservative Christian churches, women are subject to strict rules against adorning themselves. A Muslim woman covering herself with a burqa, or niqab, is similar in the sense that some religious doctrine is dictating female behavior and public appearance. What do you call that? There is a word you've used in the past."

"Legalism?"

"Yes, that's the word. It seems that no matter what faith a person may follow, human beings have a tendency to fall into legalistic thinking and practices. Sometimes, people take it to extremes."

"You know, you're right. When my father was married to his first wife early in his ministry, he used to preach a very legalistic message. In fact, he would pack the house whenever he did. In that denomination, the belief was that a person who was saved could also become unsaved by their sins. Everyone lived in fear of losing their salvation. This fear drove the women to conform to a very strict dress code. It was nothing as extreme as a burqa, but my parents spoke about 'official snippers'. Believe it or not, if a woman came to church with a feather in her hat, or with buttons on sleeves of her coat that were considered too ostentatious, the official snippers would cut them off. Of course, the women never wore makeup, but they did outrageous things with their hairstyles. The women would wear their hair up and make three buns, one on top of the other, in a way that resembled three ice cream scoops on top of somebody's head. According to my father, some members of that particular persuasion went out of their way to appear holy and sanctified on the outside, but were some of the meanest people on the inside."

"Snippers? Are you serious?"

"Yes! Then one day my father's wife went to him and said, 'I don't want to be the wife of a minister anymore.' She may have been reacting to the extremely legalistic environment of the church more than she was saying that she didn't love him. I have no way of knowing now, but my father said that she often referred to the members of this denomination as 'religious nuts'. In any case, she left my father and took their five year old daughter, Bonnie. Well, being a divorced man in that denomination meant you couldn't preach anymore. My father loved his family and wanted nothing else in life except to preach, but he left the ministry feeling condemned. He tried to sell insurance and shoes, but he was never successful in sales. For a while, before he eventually married my mother, he felt lost. Years later, I asked him why he ever chose to marry his first wife when he had told me that they were so incompatible. He answered by saying that he was often lonely growing up as the son of a physically abusive, alcoholic father who chased away his mother. He wanted a family so very badly and chose too quickly. Several days before he died, he said to me, 'I hope you never know such loneliness.' It can make you do desperate things. I believe that was why my father had such a compassionate heart. He understood the effects of suffering on a person's ability to choose well.

"When my father married my mother, some leaders of the denomination were very cruel to them. Before I was born, my mother suffered three miscarriages, which the church leaders declared to be God's judgment against my parents' marriage. My mother was heartbroken. Originally, my father bought into the legalistic theology, such as women dressing according to a code, and working to stay saved, but he was never mean-spirited. He always loved people. When he experienced firsthand the cruelty of the church leaders and the brutality of religious people, he was devastated. Bishop T.D Jakes once compared a religious beating with a Bible as worse than a physical beating by street gangs. The spirit of criticism will often use Scripture to validate self-righteousness. My father did not fit the religious system, and was criticized and ostracized. Not only did he lose his wife and daughter, but he also lost his support to minister in that denomination. He cried out to the Lord, 'Where are you, Jesus?'

"Then one day he was reading the New Testament. The scriptures that he had read many times before were now jumping off the page: *'For it is by free grace that you are saved through faith. And this salvation is not of your own doing, it came not through your own striving, but it is the gift of God; Not because of works, lest any man should boast'* (Ephesians 2:8-9). We are all saved by grace. Moreover, the Bible specifically says that we are not saved by our works or good deeds. Nothing that we can ever do, no matter how righteous we are in our own eyes, will ever win us our salvation.

"Another scripture that impressed my father so much was this: *'You have been born again, not from a mortal sperm, but from one that is immortal by the ever living and lasting Word of God'* (1 Peter 1:23). This means that when the seed of Christ is born within us, the seed cannot die. When my father began to understand the true salvation message, he pulled away from legalism. He stopped interpreting the response to his divorce as a punishment from God, and started seeing it as a release from a narrow-minded, man-made religious system that kept people in bondage. It changed his whole life and enabled him to re-establish his ministry on a new theological foundation."

I understood my father's contribution to the American church, which was the revelation of the grace of God and freedom in Christ, along with an understanding of the gifts of the spirit and corresponding fruit (1 Corinthians 12:1-27) and their expression in the life of a believer through the Holy Spirit. In that time, in the 1950's and 1960's, people were still very polarized in their beliefs about certain spiritual truths. For example, some people believed that the miracle manifestations of Christ were only possible in His time, in order to prove His deity, and not necessary or possible in our time. Jesus commissioned us Christians, however, to go and heal the sick and raise the dead (Matthew 10:8). In my father's ministry, this included the spiritually, emotionally and relationally dead, who needed a resurrection in their lives that "religion" wasn't providing. Only a divine impartation of the Holy Spirit could accomplish this. By focusing on the power and unity in Christ, my father was invited to preach in many different denominations. He believed that we could, and should do as Christ did. He who is free in Christ is free indeed (John 8:36) to follow the Holy Spirit and to exercise the ability of Christ within each one of us. *'In this love is brought to completion and attains perfection with us, that we may have confidence for the Day of Judgment because as He is, so are we in this world'* (1 John 4:17). At that time in the history of the American church, this teaching was both controversial and healing.

Legalism and grace are like oil and water. They don't mix. Either I am saved by faith in Christ and not of my works so that I can boast, or I am saved by works. Well, if I am saved by works, then which works? How many? How many sins does it take to undo the good works I have done such that God will be mad at me and send me to hell?

The Word states, *'So any person who knows what is right to do but does not do it, to him it is sin'* (James 4:17). This is the sin of omission. Does this mean that God will send me to hell for the good things I knew to do and didn't? Who makes the rule book? These questions create a lot of confusion for people. That's the problem. Some people wander around in fear of God, not reverential fear, but terror, and they run from Him. Other people are pretending to follow the rules until they are forced to face their own humanity. They throw up their hands because they realize they cannot be good enough. Then there are people who wear their spirituality with a false sense of righteousness based on superficial habits, such as covering up, or refusing to use makeup, or whatever external good works they choose. On the inside, however, they may be jealous, mean, and bitter - full of the devil. This is why Jesus said to the Pharisees, *'You are like tombs that have been whitewashed, which look beautiful on the outside but inside are full of dead men's bones and everything impure'* (Matthew 23:27).

Legalistic thinking even equates sickness with sin. When Jesus and the disciples came across a blind man, they asked Him, *'...Rabbi, who sinned, this man or his parents, that this man should be born blind'* (John 9:2)? The disciples were asking Jesus if the man's blindness was a punishment from God. Jesus answered, *'It was not that this man or his parents sinned, but he was born blind in order that the workings of God should be manifested in him'* (John 9:3). Jesus knew that He would heal the blind man to make a point about His ability to heal. Even some denominations within the contemporary church have held the belief that sickness was a punishment from God. If that were true, then we would never pray for healing. We would never go to a doctor for medicine or surgery. We should just pray to die. This makes no sense. Especially when the whole point of Jesus coming to the earth is that, through us, there would be wisdom, there would be light, there would be healing, there would be grace. We are supposed to bring the gospel, i.e. good news, to the earth.

I continued, "You know, if my father had never understood the grace message and the true nature of salvation, I wouldn't be here today."

"How's that?" my husband asked.

"Remember I told you that my mother had three miscarriages before I was born?"

"Yes."

"Well, when I was twelve, my parents told me about the unusual circumstances related to my birth. After the miscarriages, the doctor told them that they could never have children because my mother's womb was too small. This news had come the day before my father was to leave for a four week revival crusade. That night my parents made love, and my mother began to sob. He held her and cried out to God, acknowledging that He is the giver of life. My parents vowed to dedicate their child to His service if He would bless them. That was the night I was conceived. Then late in the pregnancy my mother developed toxemia, which is what she called it. Today they call it pre-eclampsia, which can cause pregnant women to go into seizures and die. I was born healthy, however, and my mother was no longer symptomatic."

"Well, I guess you were a miracle baby," my husband conceded.

"Wait. There's more to the story. When I was thirty-one, my mother developed uterine cancer. During the hysterectomy, the doctors discovered that she had two uteri, or more precisely, her uterus was divided into two compartments. One part was small and the other large. Even more confounding was that the uterus was full of active tuberculosis, which my mother originally contracted when she was eleven years old. She recovered from the infection in her lungs and lived a very healthy life. She had no idea that the TB had travelled to her uterus where it remained active until doctors discovered it when she was sixty-one. She was one of the few documented cases of active TB outside the lungs. This explained why my mother always tested positive for TB during her adult life even though the chest X-rays were always negative. Prior to her hysterectomy years later, the only explanation the doctors could give was that she was allergic to the TB test. Somehow, I never contracted the illness either in the womb or my life."

"So, let me understand. You were conceived and carried to term in a uterus that was deformed and full of TB, by a mother who could have died from seizures during pregnancy."

"That's right."

"Wow! You really were a miracle baby."

"Talk about revealing the glory of God. My birth nullified every judgment pronounced over the marriage of my parents by the legalistic elders who said my mother's womb was cursed by God. Thirty-one years later, the doctor who treated my mother for uterine cancer said to me, 'Somebody wanted you here.' My parents always told me I was born to serve the Lord. What God pronounces clean, no man can pronounce unclean!"

My husband reminded me again of the woman in the niqab. "So the woman you saw today in the store was dressed as she was based on a legalistic doctrine which says that in order to be considered good and pure, a woman must cover herself in public. And apparently different Muslim sects are debating exactly how much a woman must cover herself in order to be truly pure. How much of a woman is hidden by covering the outside, however, never tells us how good and pure the woman is on the inside, which is what God cares about. In fact, a love for Jesus would 'cover' a woman more effectively than any dress to protect her purity and righteousness."

"That's exactly right," I replied.

Jesus lived in a time dominated by legalistic thinking. In His ministry, He consistently elevated and esteemed women and freed them from legalism. Consider the situation where a woman was about to be stoned by the people of the town after they caught her in the act of adultery (John 8). Well, where was the man, and why was he not going to suffer the same punishment as the woman? Was he in the same crowd that was about to stone the woman? Jesus came along and said to the crowd, *"Let him who is without sin among you be the first to throw a stone at her."* One by one the crowd dispersed. Then he went up to the woman and wrote something in the sand, then blew it away, saying, *"I do not condemn you, either. Go on your way and from now on sin no more."* Some believe that He wrote the woman's sin in the sand. Others have speculated that he wrote the name of her sexual partner. We will never know. In any case, Jesus freed her from the responsibility for the sinful and lustful nature of men. At the same time, He directed her to be responsible for her own behavior.

Then there is the story of the woman who spent all she had on an alabaster box of expensive perfume (Matthew 26:7-13). She found Jesus eating dinner with the disciples. She knelt before Him, bathed His feet with her tears, broke open the box and anointed His feet in the perfume. She finished by wiping His feet with her hair. In just a few days, those same feet would be nailed to a cross. The disciples admonished the woman for touching Jesus and criticized her for spending so much money on perfume, money that could have been used to feed the poor. Jesus broke social protocol again and corrected them by saying, *"Why do you bother the woman? ... For you always have the poor among you, but you will not always have Me."* Jesus knew that He was going to sacrifice His life. He was accepting from this woman a final act of sacrificial love. For her sacrifice, He elevated and esteemed her in front of her critics. He stated that as long as the Gospel was to be preached, her story was to be told.

Legalism can actually kill you, if not physically then spiritually. My mother once told me that when she heard the grace message from my father and became free from legalism, she wept. She told me that previously there were days that she wished she had never heard the name of Jesus. She lived terrified of God. In her church, she would have to go every Sunday afternoon to "park meetings" where they would evangelize, sing and pray. One weekend the church leaders still made her go even though her father had just died. She could barely keep from sobbing, but the idea of missing a park meeting paralyzed her with fear. She was afraid to make God angry, even on the day that her father died. Years later, when she finally realized that God loved her and that the grace of God was sufficient to save her, she did not live a more sloppy Christian life. She fell in love with Christ all the more. At the time of my father's death, they had completed twenty-two years of fruitful ministry throughout the country. The Lord raised my father up in spite of the rejection and hateful words of "religious" people. My mother realized that Jesus became the necessary sacrifice which purchased her salvation. Serving Christ, therefore, came out of a heart of love, not of obligation or bondage. Jesus came to release us from bondage. That's the good news. That is the meaning of the word Gospel.

God does not care about my self-righteous, religious performance. He already knows everything I'm going to think before I think it. Every lustful thought. Every greedy thought. Every impatient thought. He knows every dishonest thought I may think in my life - past, present, and future. I can never cover anything up. To Him, my righteousness is as filthy rags (Isaiah 64:6). How filthy? As filthy as menstrual rags. That is God getting right to the point telling me how he considers my human attempts to do good works to earn my salvation. I can never do enough good works to earn my way to God. I do good works as an expression of my love for God, because I have experienced the power of God, and I am a vessel bringing His righteousness to the earth. This includes acts of love, goodness, kindness, mercy, and sharing the abundant life. If the good works I do were a payoff to God, then He never would have sent His Son, Jesus, to die for me. He would still hold me to the same rules that He gave to the Israelites in the Old Testament, and I would be making blood sacrifices today just as they did. Nothing would be different.

Under the dispensation of the Old Testament law, the high priest would have to make a sacrifice on the Day of Atonement. If God accepted the sacrifice, then Israel would not be judged for the sins of the previous year. God knew it was not possible for humans to keep such complex rules perfectly. That was the point. People needed a Savior. Then Jesus, the Messiah, came along. He explained that even looking upon a woman with a lustful heart was the same as committing adultery. His purpose was to encourage people to repent from the sin in their hearts before it became programmed into their behavior.

It doesn't matter, therefore, whether it is legalism in Christianity, in Islam, or in any other system created by man. The purpose of Jesus coming to the earth is to redeem my life with His sacrifice, and give me the ultimate gift of my freedom. Freedom from sin and bondage. Freedom to love and be loved. Freedom to be all that He created and called me to be. I do not have to pass inspection by everyone else to be acceptable to Him. In the end, it is His acceptance that matters. When I fall in love with Christ and yield myself to Him, God begins the transformation inside of me. He writes His will on my heart. I become a bond slave. This is a slave that chooses to remain with the Master who has already freed him. A bond slave stays and serves willingly because of love. My behavior is constrained by love, not by a tyrannical master.

I own the responsibility to manage my thoughts and make good choices. I am accountable for my life. I have been purchased by the blood of Jesus and am totally accepted by Him. I have access to God's love and salvation through Jesus, just like anyone else. This means that, with Christ in me, I can be free from the bondage of sin. In the end, other people have no power over me. Jesus said, *"Do not be afraid of those who can kill the body but cannot kill the soul; but rather be afraid of Him who can destroy both soul and body in hell"* (Matthew 10:28). This life is not the end of everything. It is only the beginning. As Jesus said to Pilate, I believe the same is true for us today: *"You would not have any power or authority against Me if it were not given you from above"* (John 19:11). Human beings do not define me, nor do they have any spiritual authority over me unless I allow it. Once I receive this revelation, it frees me to fulfill my divine purpose, love others and relate to them with the same understanding.

Some people who manifest a religious spirit and show no grace have never been taught about the grace of God or experienced it for themselves. Others are under such a wet blanket of condemnation that they are unable to receive it. They cannot give you what they do not understand or what they do not have. People who fight the message of grace refer to it as "sloppy agape", and maintain that if they were to accept total freedom in Jesus Christ, they would live an undisciplined life. If you could live your life with no restraint and no conviction of sin, then I would be concerned about your relationship with Him in the first place. Liberty is not a license to act without restraint. Rules without relationship always ends in rebellion.

Jesus was the substitute for all of my sins. When He said, *"It is finished!"* (John 19:30), He meant it. He has promised that He will finish the work that He started in me.

Abba Father, freedom is so precious. Thank You for giving me the privilege to be called Your daughter. You claim me as Your own. The world expects me to conform in order to receive love and acceptance. Just about the time I think I know the rules, somebody is quick to let me know that I do not measure up. It is frustrating and heartbreaking.

There were times when I was trying to keep up appearances. I believed that if I ever let my guard down and showed my humanity, people I loved would walk away. Some have. I thought You would walk away also because I disappointed You. I am sorry that I misjudged You.

I am not proud of all the decisions and actions in my life. Salvation is instant, but sanctification will be an ongoing process. I am grateful that You see the "real me" and You do not run away. You see me down to the core of my being, and still decided that I was worth it for You to send Jesus to die for me.

I am relieved to know that I do not have to impress You with my good works. I live to express Your love to others, because I am the recipient of that love. This is my motivation. The more I grow to understand the breath and the depth of Your love for me, the easier it is to let go of behaviors, attitudes and desires that displease You. I submit to Your will and ways because I trust in that love. You will never keep anything or anyone from me that is in my best interest.

Faith without works is dead. Your Word says that without faith, it is impossible to please You, or complete the works You want to do through me. Anything I do without faith in You is worthless. You save me. You sanctify me. You complete me.

Help me to quit striving to please. Instead, help me to relax in Your presence, completely safe in Your unending, abiding, and transforming love. Only when I fully let myself fall into Your arms of grace, will I then be able to stand up and become mature in You. My behavior will begin to manifest Your likeness. I will not need to bow down to the form of religious systems or cultural expectations. My choices will flow out of my freedom in You. Behavior modification is not spiritual transformation. I want to experience authentic change in my life.

Forgive me for ever being guilty of looking down the long side of my nose in judgment of someone else. Help me instead to pray for them all the while understanding, that I am just as human. Deliver me from any self-righteous, religious spirit.

You have freed me. I am no longer in bondage. I am no longer afraid.

I pray and confess all these things as so, in the matchless, incomparable name of Jesus Christ. Amen.

Makeup Lesson 6: Serums

($$$) Skin aging is a dual process involving both genetics and environment. The visible signs of aging are a loss of firmness and smoothness, dark spots and discolorations, and the formation of lines and wrinkles. On a cellular level, metabolism decreases, causing cells to produce less of the essential proteins needed to maintain skin's structure. Damaged DNA may result in either alteration of the cells' ability to produce needed components for healthy looking skin, or even premature cell death.

The prestige lines boast a variety of serums designed to address skin issues on a cellular level. Each serum serves a different purpose. Some serums target the loss of luminosity in the skin due to loss of protein as we age. These serums also retexturize the skin by smoothing pores, wrinkles and fine lines. Other serums can reduce the appearance of sun damage, age spots, freckles, and discolorations. Certain serums assist with maintaining collagen levels in the skin for a firmer and more radiant look. Existing lines will be visibly diminished, giving skin a brighter and more youthful look. There are even serums to reduce the redness and the appearance of minor scars. Certain serums cater specifically to sensitive skin, while others have vitamins and anti-oxidants.

Apply serums twice per day, both morning and night. First, cleanse and tone your face. Then follow with your eye regimen. After that, use the serum. A small amount typically goes a long way. You will gently pat the product onto the skin and then gently massage it into the face in an upward, never downward, motion.

There are also serums for the body, which are extremely beneficial if you have very dry, itchy skin caused by a variety of factors. Serums are a wonderful addition to a regimen. Normal skin will appear healthy, radiant, hydrated, and plump. Use serums not to replace moisturizers, but in addition to them.

Lesson #7

Spirit to Spirit

I had been working now for four months. Although I was hired primarily for one particular line, as clients needed help I would also sell products from other lines. Because I was doing well with my sales, management offered me a position as the counter manager with one of the other prestige lines with the objective of increasing sales in that line. There was no counter manager at the time. In this store, this product line had been neglected and was not performing to its potential. My responsibility would be to increase sales. I had started to earn some decent commissions in my current role because of the established customer base. It was a risk, therefore, to give that up and take over a neglected line, even if I was given a raise in my base. My decision was easy to make because I did not consider this part-time position my career. I was still anticipating that I would be moving on to pursue my passion project full-time any month now, so I took the position.

Besides moving from one line to another, I also moved physically to the center of the cosmetics department in this store. All the cosmetics bays for the other lines were arranged around my line, similar to the spokes of a wheel. This gave me the opportunity to have better access to all the women in the cosmetics department. While I was not aware of it at the time, I realized that this was exactly God's plan. He had an agenda. There are no accidents with God. Everything is according to His sovereign plan when you are committed to Him.

At the same time, another woman had recently been promoted to manage yet another prestige line. In my new location, I had more time to get to know her. Her name was Cassie. She was vivacious with short brown hair and beautiful green eyes. She and I had a lot in common.

"Where did you grow up, Cassie?"

"In Jackson, Mississippi," Cassie answered, revealing her Southern accent. "I don't like going back there. I had a tough childhood."

"How so?" I asked cautiously.

"Well, my father was my hero. I loved him so much, but he was ill my entire childhood. Crohn's disease. There's no cure for it, and he made it worse by smoking, but I don't think he understood that at the time."

"I understand. My father was my hero, too, and he was also sick as far back as I can remember. He had Lupus. There were times he couldn't get out of bed, but he was a preacher and a pianist. When it was time for him to preach and play, miracles happened! God did amazing things through him."

"Sounds as though you loved him a great deal."

"Yes, I did."

"Do you have any brothers and sisters, Peggy?"

"Well, yes, a half sister, but she died when I was a teenager. I didn't meet her until after my father died. Her name was Bonnie. She was fifteen years older than me. After her mother's death, she discovered the letters our father had sent to her over the years. Her mother had hidden them from her in a safe deposit box. When she finally understood that our father had not abandoned her, but really loved her, she tried to find him. Unfortunately, she was two months too late. She was devastated that he had died before she could talk to him, but I was thrilled to talk to my older sister. Two weeks later, Bonnie came to visit my mother and me in New York City. We had a magical weekend together and quickly became very close. We had all these plans about how we were going to make up for lost time, but she died only a year and a half after that visit. She was visiting friends who had a summer home. She was swimming in the river with several other people when she drowned suddenly. She went under the water to push the hair back from her face, and she never came back up. The doctor said she died from a brain aneurism. I was devastated. Her uncanny resemblance to my father made her death harder for me to bear. It was like having him die all over again. I thought she and I would have a lifetime to make up for lost memories, but suddenly she was gone."

"I'm sorry to hear that," Cassie interjected. "That's as sad as my story. When I was twelve, my sister and I were riding home from school on our bikes. She rode ahead of me and turned the corner and was out of my sight. Suddenly, I heard screeching brakes and a crash. A few seconds later I rode up to the corner and saw my sister on the road, bleeding. Her bike was a mangled mess. I was screaming. My sister was pronounced dead at the scene."

"Oh, my God!"

"Yeah! It devastated my mother. Here she was trying to take care of my father, never expecting to lose her daughter. I don't know if my mother ever truly got over my sister's death. We were never close after that. My father had been my best friend. I adored him. In my mother's eyes, however, it seemed I could never do anything right."

"So, we were both made 'only children' in our teenage years with widowed mothers who used to be caregivers."

Cassie and I clearly had a lot in common. We became fast friends. I could relate to Cassie's whole life. It is so difficult for a child to grow up with a parent who is terminally ill. First, you understand at a very young age that life is very fragile. When other kids are out playing and being silly, you are dealing with life and death issues all the time. You know that someone you love might not be there tomorrow. Then, when you deal with unexpected tragedy, such as the death of a sibling, it rocks your world. Old people are supposed to die, not young people. You ask yourself, "Why did she die and why did I live?" This puts incredible pressure on a child to fill in the missing pieces for other family members. Cassie felt a lot of pressure to be something for her mother that she could never be. No matter what she ever did, or how good she would be, she could never replace the daughter who was lost. Cassie's mother was never warm toward Cassie after the death of her sister. My own mother loved me fiercely but was often very stern with me after the death of my father. I attributed her behavior to the fact that she did not want to risk getting too close to me, in case she lost me, too. How could she survive that? I suggested to Cassie that her own mother may have reacted the same way.

Whenever we were scheduled to work at the same time, we would find time to confide in each other and learned more about how our lives had followed similar paths. Cassie is about ten years younger than me. Like me, she was married for the second time. She has a daughter and son from her first marriage. The son is a young adult now. The daughter was in high school. My mother had passed about ten years ago, but Cassie's mother was living now near Jackson with her stepfather.

One evening when business in the store was slow, I went over to Cassie. "How are you tonight?"

"Exhausted!"

"How come?"

"Last night my mother called me at four in the morning."

"What happened?"

"Nothing happened. My mother has Alzheimer's. This isn't the first time she's called me early in the morning. She's often confused and doesn't know what time it is. Last night she was sure that there was a strange man in her house. I had to explain to her for 45 minutes that the strange man was her husband. Last year when she came with my stepdad to visit, she thought my daughter, her granddaughter, was my son's girlfriend. She's giving my stepdad fits. He's a saint. He's taking great care of her, but she has accused him of all sorts of things, like having an affair. It's been terrible, but believe it or not, if she were to walk up to this counter right now you would think she was delightful."

"I know what that's like. My Aunt Jackie had dementia. I remember one time when my husband and I picked her up from the senior home to take her to church and then to lunch. We sat down and were having a pleasant time eating our meal. My husband decided to try to engage her in some adult conversation by asking her about the upcoming presidential election between senators McCain and Obama. 'Who are you going to vote for, Jackie?' he asked. She looked up and said, 'Oh, I don't know. I'm thinkin' about Lincoln!' We were practically choking on our food from laughing so hard. Poor Jackie didn't even know what she had said, but she started laughing, too.

"On the other hand," I continued, "there were times that she would be enraged and accuse me of the craziest things. There is actually a term for that. It's called Sundowner's. People with dementia may at times appear pleasant and lucid during the day, but then become confused and agitated at night. It was horrible to look at the hatred for me in Jackie's eyes when she was accusing me of terrible things, knowing all along she was confusing me with her biological sister whom she hadn't seen in years."

Cassie continued, "Well, my mother was diagnosed with Alzheimer's six months ago, and she has declined quickly. Here I am in Dallas, and I can't go home to help her and my stepdad. I've been thinking about quitting this job to move back to Jackson, but I just got this promotion. If I went back to Jackson, my daughter would have to stay here with her father and I wouldn't get to see her finish high school. My mother wouldn't know I was there anyway. I don't know what to do.

"Help me, Peggy! I don't know how to pray. I don't want my mother to live like this, and I don't want to see her go into a nursing home. I feel as though I am asking God for my mother's death. What does that make me? Am I being selfish?"

I could see that Cassie was struggling. These were hard questions. Alzheimer's is a terrible disease because those who suffer from it can live for years. Her mother was still relatively young in her mid-60's and in very good health. She could realistically live another 20 years. Cassie appreciated her stepdad's devotion to her mother, but he was in his 70's. How long could he manage to take care of her mother before someone had to take care of him? Cassie was facing the agony so many adults will face as Alzheimer's grows into an epidemic in this country.

"Cassie, I believe you want to pray for God to have mercy on your mother. Can God heal your mother? I believe that yes, He can heal the body and the mind. He is the great Physician, but if God doesn't heal your mother, you don't want her to suffer, of course. You don't want to be fearful, either. Alzheimer's may have a genetic link. I've read that there are things that we can do now to prevent or delay to onset of Alzheimer's, such as doing puzzles, learning languages or music, and exercising. A healthful diet may also make a difference. Scripture teaches that, *'God did not give us a spirit of timidity, but of power and of love and of calm and well-balanced mind and discipline and self-control'* (2 Timothy 1:7). I believe that you and I can stand on that scripture and pray for ourselves and your mother. We need to do what we can do now to preserve our own mental health."

Like me, Cassie was a nurturer. She had also been a single parent. The combination can be crippling for women in particular when loved ones expect them to have the right answer all the time. It's easier to fix things for children when they are small. Kids believe that moms can kiss the pain away. It is harder when children grow up and make mistakes.

It was another night when we were working together that Cassie came to me.

"Peggy, can I talk to you?"

"What is it, Cassie?"

"My nineteen year old son is making very poor choices."

"What happened?"

"He was going to a party last weekend with this girl, not really a girlfriend. They stopped at a store with the intention of getting some cigarettes, beer, and wine for the party. According to my son, the girl gave him a credit card to buy the alcohol. She said the card belonged to her boyfriend. Turns out she lied. She had stolen it. I know this because the police came to my house yesterday to question my son. How could he do something so foolish? It's as though he's lost his mind. I think I'm losing my mind! Ugghh!!"

"I know, Cassie. There were times I felt the same way."

My own children struggled with abandonment issues. My son and I had a great relationship when he was younger. Then, after the divorce, I had to work, and his father wasn't around. It was so hard to keep everything in balance. I started getting calls from school saying he was hanging around with the wrong kids. I spent so much time being frightened for him. There are no perfect parents, and there are no perfect children.

Years have passed, and although my children have been through deep water, God continues to be faithful. I am turning the care and burden of them over to Him. He continues to use different means with each child to get their attention. I pray that someday my children will come to understand how much He loves them, and will give Him a chance to heal all their wounds. I wish it would have been easier on us, but there is power in praying for your children. I believe it is what parents are called to do. My parents prayed for me every day, and I believe they are still praying for me.

As we finished talking, Cassie said to me, "Peggy, thank you so much for listening to me. I have no one else to talk to." I realized that I had been like Cassie much of my life, unable to express what was going on with me and my life, with few around that I thought would understand me. I believed that God had me there to be a friend to Cassie, someone who was empathetic and non-judgmental. He was also calling me to intercede in prayer on her behalf.

There were times I was concerned about her because she had told me that she was having trouble with high blood pressure. One evening in particular I saw this dazed look in her face. I had brought Cassie a book of prayers and gave it to her. "Cassie, I want you to know I am praying for you."

"Oh, Peggy!" She looked at me with desperation in her face.

"What is it, Cassie?"

"My husband is in serious trouble."

"What?! Where? Why?"

"I'm not sure. He told me he was going to see a friend out of state, someone he's known since childhood. They got involved in some sort of business deal, and his friend deceived him."

"Oh, no!"

"What am I going to do? We're in the middle of a legal hornet's nest. He never told me about the deal. I don't understand any of it. His mother is mortgaging her house to help us pay for an attorney." She started to cry.

"Cassie, has he ever done anything like this before?"

"No, never. It doesn't make any sense. He said that he thought this opportunity would help us get out of debt."

"Are you sure he's telling you the whole truth?"

"I… I think so. I mean, I love him. He's a good man. I believe he loves me. He has never done anything to hurt me, but everything seems to be caving in on top of me."

"I understand more than you know, sweetie. I have gone into business with people I thought were my friends. I'll never do that again. God's grace will be sufficient to get you through this. I'll be here to pray with you. Until then, I recommend you keep asking him to explain what happened until you're satisfied you know the truth.

"Cassie, understand this. Marriage contracts are broken and violated every day, but a marriage covenant requires both husband and wife to be transparent with each other. I am less concerned about the business deal that went wrong and more concerned about the fact that you knew nothing about it. You may have to ask yourself some very hard questions and get some answers to them. As you pray, the Lord will reveal truth to you."

"Peggy, after I got that call from my husband, I couldn't sleep. I was wandering around my apartment screaming and crying out to God, 'God, I'll do what You want me to do, but I don't know how to pray. I don't know what You want from me! Everyone around me is acting crazy! What am I supposed to do?'

"Peggy, what do I do?"

"The only thing you *can* do, Cassie. You have to get a word from God. Most people don't know that they can even get a word from God; that He will speak to you. On top of that, Cassie, people don't know *how* to get a word from God. What is He going to do, speak in an audible voice? Well, I guess He can if He wants, but since we already have the Word of God in the Scriptures, He doesn't typically reveal Himself and speak to people the way He did in the Old Testament."

For me it became very simple to understand how to get a word from God. A baby learns to speak by listening to its mother. English is my "mother tongue." French is the mother tongue of someone born to parents in France, and so forth.

What is the language of God? How does God speak to us? Well, God in another form is the Holy Spirit. God is a Spirit. You have a spirit. In the same way, I would speak to you with my voice using language, God speaks to us Spirit to spirit.

So then, how does the spirit sound? I think we know it all the time. When God speaks to us, we sometimes call it intuition. It's something my father used to call your "Knower". After he would seek God in prayer, he would say, "I know in my Knower." He had an awareness deep down inside that he could not fully explain, yet was certain he knew and understood. A secular term for intuition is emotional intelligence. Experts in this field maintain that the most successful people in life are often not the most brilliant intellectually, but those that have the emotional intelligence to perceive events and people or discern opportunities around them and know what to do with them.

I believe this intuition, this quiet voice inside you, is the voice of God answering you when you pray. When you ask the question, "Father, should I go here, or should I do that?" He will answer you with a pull or a drawing in a certain direction that gives you a sense of rightness about the situation, or a sense of caution.

I explained all this to Cassie, and I continued, "There are no easy answers for the storms in your life, except that you pray and ask God to give you peace about what you are doing, or intend to do. If, for example, you feel restless about moving to Jackson to be with your mother, and you have prayed until God releases you to go, then you go. God will give you peace and grace to move in that direction. If, on the other hand, you do not feel released to move to Jackson, then there is no condemnation on you for following the answer God gives to you."

I never had to question my father's voice whenever he called me. I knew my father's voice. I recognized the sound of it. I also knew what to expect from him when he would speak to me. At the same time, I knew what he would never say to me. No one could fool me with my father's voice. The most important thing I knew is that my father loved me. He was never going to tell me something that was not in my best interest.

How much more clear would the heavenly Father be with you? You will know His voice. You just may not be recognizing that it is God within you speaking to you. The more you yield to His voice, the more you will recognize it, and the more He will speak to you. I describe it as thoughts that bypass your brain. He impresses you with specific instruction and it's just something you know you have to do. You trust it. There will be confirmation in His Word. He'll never tell you to do something that is not consistent with Scripture. For example, He is never going to tell you to go out and have an affair because it would be good for your marriage. Why? Because He has given a commandment against adultery. If you ever feel pulled in the direction to have an affair, or commit any sin, then it is not the voice of God.

Cassie focused her eyes intently on me as I continued ministering to her. "At the same time, the Word is not going to answer you explicitly by saying, 'Thou shalt move to Mississippi when your mother has Alzheimer's.' So how do you get an answer? You learn to listen to that still, small voice inside of you. Sometimes it is not a still voice; sometimes it's a fire alarm. When you make decisions without praying and waiting to hear His inner voice, you will end up making the wrong choice.

"The key is you have to be willing to tune out what people would impose upon you. There are some who would criticize your stepfather severely for putting your mother in a nursing home. I know how that feels. You are caught in a situation for which there is no good solution, and you are drowning. Usually these people sitting in judgment of you have never walked where you walk. They have no clue how it feels when you can't sleep because you're afraid that your mother may wander outside the house during the night. No one is capable of staying up twenty-four hours a day, seven days a week in order to supervise someone. Your stepfather, Cassie, is currently shouldering that responsibility. Also, the cost of private duty health care to avoid a nursing facility is astronomical. Very few people can afford that."

"This makes sense, Peggy. I understand. Thank you, again, for listening and understanding me."

"You're welcome, honey. I will be praying for you, your mother and your stepfather. I know it's a heartbreaking situation."

"Yes, please. Thank you so much!"

After our shift, we said good night to each other. A few days later we were working together again. Cassie came up to me.

"Last night an ambulance came to pick up my mother and take her to a psychiatric hospital. She was hurting herself. She was convinced that there was something in her mouth and was cutting herself while looking in the mirror. She wouldn't stop even after she started bleeding. My stepfather told me that after she recovers in the hospital he is going to place her directly into a nursing home.

"I have to thank you, Peggy. I was able to share with my stepfather the things you shared with me, and tell him that I didn't blame him. I told him that I knew he loved her and wouldn't harm her. I told him that I felt relieved that she would be watched and cared for around the clock. We won't have to worry about her leaving the house and getting lost, or worse."

"I'm sorry about your mother, Cassie, but I'm glad to hear that God has provided a solution," I assured her.

"Peggy, I've decided that I'm the only person responsible for my life. I've got to get my blood pressure under control. So, I'm going to start eating better. Yesterday, I went to the gym for the first time in a long time. It's tough to exercise when you work retail, but I know this is something I have to do. I am just going to commit to going regardless of how tired I feel."

As I listened to Cassie, I realized that this was an act of redemption in my life. God was redeeming the suffering I had experienced in my life. The Scripture says, *"Blessed be the God and Father of our Lord Jesus Christ, the Father of sympathy and the God of every comfort, who comforts us in every trouble, so that we may also be able to comfort those who are in any kind of trouble or distress, with the comfort with which we ourselves are comforted by God"* (2 Corinthians 1:3-4). There was purpose in it all. When I started to look at my whole life, the wonderful and the tragic, I could see the tapestry that God was weaving from my life. Of course, when I was in the middle of it, I could see only the backside. It was a knotted mess. For many years, I often thought, *When is this bloodbath going to end?*

Based on our conversations and the encouragement I gave her to hear the voice of God, Cassie was now able to tell me something that she believed God was saying to her:

"This is not your fight."

"You need to give that child to Me."

"My grace will sustain you through this lawsuit."

"You were never meant to be your mother's husband."

"You were meant to be your mother's daughter."

"You were never supposed to be the sacrificial lamb. The only sacrificial lamb was My Son. I sent Jesus for that purpose. You are not equipped to handle that role. You must give everyone you love to Me."

The best gift a person can give to another believer is to teach them how to get a word from God on their own. There is no benefit to a person who tries to hitchhike on anyone else's spiritual experience. Any person who looks to you to be their spiritual answer man from God is practicing a form of idolatry. No one can become the voice of God for another. God never wants this. You should not want it, either. Yes, God will call people to study the Word, teach, and preach. We get instruction from spiritual leaders and usually find them in church. There is nothing wrong with this. Iron does sharpen iron. There are also certain people who are gifted with a word of wisdom and knowledge from God. When someone gives you a "word from God" for your life, it will resonate inside of you when they speak. Even if it is something you do not want to do or has never occurred to you, it will bear witness in your spirit. It may not even be new information. Nevertheless, it will be the answer you have been seeking from God. This is not the same as going to a medium.

When I am in a particularly difficult place, I ask God to confirm it to me through multiple sources. In one particular situation, I was seeking God as to whether or not I was to leave a certain place or to stay. It seemed as though everywhere I turned I would hear the same scripture: *"<u>Be still</u> and know that I am God"* (Psalm 46:10). For example, I would go to church and hear it in the sermon. Then, I would turn on the television and listen to a minister share the same scripture. Next, I would turn on the radio, and the same thing would happen. Finally, I would open a devotional book at random and read the same scripture. By then I was convinced to be still, and not leave.

Once I was in a potentially dangerous place when a friend of mine came to me very sweetly and said, "Peggy, I know you believe that God has told you to stay and be still, but what does that mean? There are those of us around you who love you and are concerned for your well being. Would you please go to God and ask Him again?"

I said, "Of course I will. I'm truly doing what I believe God has instructed me to do, even though it makes no sense. I am not trying to alarm anyone or harm myself."

That day, when she left, I said, "Lord, please help me. I need You to show me if I am staying here in Your will or if you want me to leave."

Within moments after this prayer, I had what I would describe as a daydream. In my mind's eye, I saw myself walking down this beautiful country road with the sunlight filtering through the trees. I suddenly looked down and saw a snake coiled at my feet hissing angrily at me. Naturally, I froze. It was so menacing and terrifying. The Lord spoke very clearly again in my spirit. It was as though He was communicating to the DNA of my being. I just knew the meaning of what He was conveying by the images I was seeing in my mind. It is clear that in nature, with some deadly adversaries, the worst thing you can do is to move. You must remain perfectly still. In my 'daydream', I could barely hear myself breathing. The snake looked at me and eventually slithered into the bushes. I continued to walk straight ahead.

I knew in my "Knower" at that moment that God was telling me that I was not to move. He was going to cause my adversary to move away from me. That is exactly what happened. The enemy kept giving me opportunities to take action, but I knew that I was not to initiate any closure.

In 2007, my husband and I went on an Alaskan cruise with his family. We took a train ride through the Denali Park. While we were going through the park, I learned fascinating facts about bears. There are two types of bears in the wild. Some are black bears, and some are brown. If you ever encounter a black bear in the wild, you should stand your ground and fight back. If you see a brown bear, you should play dead and remain perfectly still. Your survival depends on knowing your adversary.

Out of all the vegetation in a forest, bears coming out of hibernation can distinguish between a poisonous and non-poisonous plant to find the berries they need to eat as a laxative. How do bears know which plant? God never created a bear in His image, and never sent Jesus to die for a bear's sins. Yet, He provided for the bear's existence and well-being. How much more is God interested in providing for your existence and well-being? The first step is that you have to believe He will speak to you, and you will hear Him. Scripture teaches, *"The sheep that are My own hear and are listening to My voice, and I know them, and they follow Me"* (John 10:27).

You cannot hear God unless you are in relationship with Him and His son, Jesus Christ. Jesus said, *"I am the Way and the Truth and the Life; no one comes to the Father except through Me"* (John 14:6). To be in relationship with God, therefore, requires that you accept Christ as your Savior. As the Word says, *"If you acknowledge and confess with your lips that Jesus is Lord and in your heart believe that God raised Him from the dead, you will be saved"* (Romans 10:9). All you have to do is ask Him to come into your heart and believe that He died for you, taking your place to give you access to God. You have the Holy Spirit within you. His Spirit will "bear witness" with your spirit when you hear something. He will communicate to you and you will know it.

When you develop a close relationship with Christ, and you spend time in His word, and in praise and worship, you do not desire to go against His leading. Your flesh may struggle with His instructions at times, but you will never be comfortable with disobedience. It will not set well with you.

The written Word of God is available to everyone, but when it comes to life questions, such as, "Should I leave my job and go to Mississippi?" you need a Rhema word from God. When you are in close relationship with Him, He gives you a Rhema word of specific instruction that is "burning bush" clear. You learn as a child to ask "why?" when you don't understand something. If you recognize the sovereignty of God, however, sometimes you should neither seek an explanation from God, nor give one to others about your actions in response to His word. When He is intimately involved in every aspect of your life, then His Word will always be in your best interest, even though it may make no more sense than when He told Jehoshaphat to send out the singers first against three nations attacking Israel at the same time (2 Chronicles 20). While the singers where praising and worshiping God, the enemy armies attacked and slaughtered each other. Israel did no fighting. After the battle, it took three days for Israel to collect all the plunder from the defeated armies.

When God gives you direction, you will experience supernatural peace and grace. If you feel no peace or grace, then either God has not answered yet, or you are uncertain about His answer, or you are disobeying His instructions. Learning to hear from God is a skill you can learn, if you will submit to the process. If you are uncertain, then stop what you are doing and wait for Him to confirm His direction. If you are acting in disobedience, then repent. When you therefore act on a proceeding word from Him, no other human has the right to sit in judgment of you. No one else is qualified to judge you because they have not walked where you walk. God is the only one can sit in judgment.

When you are faced with challenges that weaken your knees or break your heart, the question is, what does God want? What does God expect of women like Cassie and me and the other women in the cosmetics department? What is He expecting of you in this moment of your life? There are so many women that are heads of households and so many fathers who are absent. I believe that you must choose to redefine yourself and your life by resisting the unrealistic expectations that surround you. Your identity is secured in Christ and defined by an unconditionally loving God who promises to be your peace and provision.

Women are notorious for fighting and competing with each other. What would happen, however, if they would drop their swords and link arms with each other, just as the women have done in this cosmetics department? Here, we have been vulnerable enough to say, "I'm weeping over my own sorrow, but I can have empathy for your sorrow, too." We have gone a step further to say, "I'm not just going to cry with you, I'm also going to grab you by the hand and take you to the only One who can dry your tears and give you a new direction." In this way, we have moved together from a position of feeling helpless to a position of being truly powerful.

Abba Father, I confess that, at times, I have felt very confused, hurt, and angry with You. I felt as though You were up there sitting on Your hands, when You could have done something to stop the heartache and prevent the tragedies in my life. Now I understand that much of the time I have been wandering around in the mess of my own creation. I have suffered from my own choices that were not in Your will for me.

I have not always known how to hear You. There were so many voices in the land. There have also been unfortunate circumstances that happened to me through no fault of my own. It has taken me a long time to sift through the chaos in order to understand how much was my responsibility, and how much was the result of living in a fallen world.

Father, I am sorry for not listening better. Forgive me for my open rebellion and sin. Cover me with Your mercy and grace. Give me the strength to endure the process of walking out the consequences of my behavior.

Help me to forgive those who have trespassed against me. Their betrayal has cost me greatly and my wounds still sting. I now comprehend that when I sin against You, it stings Your heart, as well. I have been the recipient of your boundless grace. Teach me to be an instrument of that same grace.

Make Yourself "burning bush" clear to me as You did with Moses when You told him to go back to Egypt, the place from which he had run from the consequences of his sin. You spoke in such a way that he knew without a shadow of a doubt that it was Your instruction. I need You to confirm Your instructions to me. Some of the decisions I must make affect not only my life, but also the lives of those I love. They may never understand me or agree with me. Help me to have the strength to obey You, regardless of whether it makes sense to me or anyone else.

Your peace will be my umpire. Regardless of how desperate my situation may appear, I will not move until I hear You. Then I will act with confidence and boldness, knowing that You have already gone before me to clear the way.

Thank You, Father, for hearing me when I pray. I ask this in the precious name of Jesus and for His sake, Amen. So be it!

Makeup Lesson 7: Eye Creams and Treatments

($$) The common concerns women voice about their eyes are wrinkles, sagging skin or loss of firmness, puffiness, crepeiness around the upper lid, dark circles, and loss of eyelashes and eyebrows. The prestige lines have targeted treatments for each of these issues, but they have to be applied correctly.

Eye treatments include serums and creams. After you cleanse and tone your face, the eye treatment should be applied next in sequence. This is a very important step. Eye treatments are ophthalmologically tested and will create a barrier for the other products to be placed on the face that are not tested. Clients often return eye products saying that it burned their eyes. While this may be true in some cases, it is not the fault of the product in general. The fault usually is in the application.

Apply eye creams and serums with the pinky finger or the ring finger. Do not apply great pressure to sensitive eye areas. Take a cue tip and place four small dots around the cheek bone area and then above the eye by the brow bone. The rule is "if it's not on the bone, leave it alone." Your eye is a heat sensitive organ, and it will naturally pull the product toward the eye. You must be careful where you place the product. It will not blind you, but it may irritate your eyes. Once applied properly, proceed with the application of other makeup products.

Some women struggle with the loss of eyebrows and lashes because of aging, hormonal changes, thyroid changes or chemotherapy. There are products that encourage the growth of eyelashes and eyebrows. When using these products, trace the eyelash line on the top and bottom as well as the brows along the existing hairline. You may see results in two to four weeks, as long as the follicle is not completely dead. Some of these products will not cause a change of color to the skin above the eye area and are not as costly as those treatments prescribed by a doctor. This is more cost effective than the current alternative, which are eyelash extensions. Follow product directions and repeat this process every two to three weeks. Use mascara on the bottom lashes only as needed.

Lesson #8

Beauty in Every Woman

It was Christmas time. This was the best time of year to make good commissions. Management had challenged me to increase sales, but was very slow in making the investment in inventory that I thought was needed to accomplish this objective. Compared to last year, however, my numbers were up, and I was working more hours. I was glad for the extra money, as well as for the opportunities I continued to have to pray for both clients and other consultants.

I was standing by my bay with a sea of people around me. Christmas music was playing, and the atmosphere was loud and festive. I turned around when a woman called to me. She raised her voice above the background noise, saying, “Excuse me, ma’am! Would you be so kind as to give my mother a makeover?”

I answered, “Of course, I would be happy to do that.” Her mother was behind her, and I didn’t see her until after I answered. I felt instantly ill. Her face was covered with growths. They were fleshy, wart-like cysts. In a vain attempt to cover the growths, she had applied an extremely dark brown foundation over her fair complexion. At first glance, I was shocked. Nevertheless, I showed her mother to my chair and asked her to have a seat while I went to get my brushes. I walked around the other side of the bay and desperately called out under my breath, “Jesus, please help me! This woman is clearly ill, and I don’t want anything to register on my face that would embarrass her.” In that instant, it seemed as though God snapped His fingers, and this rush of grace came over me. I knew that God had sent her to me. When I looked into her eyes, I knew something was wrong. She had no awareness of how she looked. It reminded me of my sweet Aunt Jackie when she had dementia.

I asked her, “What is your name, ma’am?”

“My name is Martha,” she replied.

Her daughter, who was standing close by, spoke lovingly of her mother. “Mother lives in an assisted-living center now. I’m a nurse and we’re visiting for the holidays from Oklahoma. Our family is having a portrait done tomorrow, and I want to treat my mother to some new makeup.”

I said, "Miss Martha, I am going to have to take all your makeup off so I can prepare your face with the appropriate skincare."

"That's fine, dear."

I had to use my hands and put cream all over her face, touching these terrible growths. While I was doing this, I began to realize that the other consultants would have found a way to avoid this awkward situation. It was Christmas. They were too busy serving clients - a perfectly legitimate reason. My line was slow; I didn't have any excuse. God did not want me to have an excuse. He wanted me to love on this very ill lady, and minister to her daughter.

I don't think the daughter expected me to do the makeover. I think she wanted someone else to help her mother understand that the dark brown foundation on her fair skin was wrong. I understand how it is to tell someone who is confused in their mind that they are mistaken. They cannot and sometimes will not hear you. It is horrible to have to parent your parent because they have lost the ability to comprehend reality. In my experience, elderly family members will take the truth from strangers before they will take it from their child, even when their child is an adult who is trying to look out for them.

I felt as though Miss Martha's daughter needed me to do that for her. In my spirit, I knew that God wanted me to give this woman a complete makeover. I looked at her hands and saw the dark bruising that was a sure sign of impending death. As I worked on Miss Martha, her daughter was standing behind her with tears in her eyes, mouthing the words, "Thank you so much." I winked at her and smiled back.

No amount of makeup on this woman was going to change her visible disfigurement. When I finished, I could tell that she felt beautiful, as though she could not see the growths on her face that were still readily noticeable.

"Well, Miss Martha, let's see how you look. How do you feel?"

She was so excited. "Oh, my goodness! How beautiful! You do wonderful work, dear. Thank you so much! Look at me, hun." She was talking now to her daughter. "What do you think?"

When I wrapped up, she started ordering every product that we used in the makeover. I gracefully tried to explain the cost of the items. In my heart, I believed that she would not live long enough to use them all. Her daughter said, "It's all right. If my mama wants it, she can have it."

I said, "Miss Martha, I have so enjoyed getting to know you and your daughter today. I will be praying for you. I serve a great God who loves you."

Her eyes filled with tears. Her daughter hugged me. I gave her some samples and told her to take care of herself. I know how being a caregiver can be emotionally, physically, and spiritually draining. It is heartbreaking to try to care for your loved one who does not want your help or believe it is necessary.

When they walked away, I knew that when I cried out to God, He filled my hands, my fingers, my eyes, and my smile with His presence. He touched that woman through me. Many years ago, I performed a song called "Holy Spirit Touch Through Me", by The SevenMidnight. Little did I know that twenty-five years later God would answer the prayer of that song for this woman in a cosmetics department. Martha needed to understand that she could not become disfigured enough for God not to want to touch her through one of His children. The lyrics go as follows:

Touch through me, Holy Spirit. Touch through me.
Let my hands reach out to others. Touch through me.
There's a lonely soul somewhere, needing just one friend to care.
So, touch through me, Holy Spirit. Touch through me.

Sometimes people live in denial. They go to extremes to camouflage the outbreak of sin or pain in their lives, believing that others are oblivious to it also. They may be so blinded by deception that they do not see the obvious, glaring truth.

Other people may not be in denial, but still prefer to avoid exposure. For example, women who come to the counter will hesitate when I offer to demonstrate a new color on their face. For whatever reason, they will refuse to let me take off their makeup. People have a tendency to be more protective of the skin on their face than the skin on the rest of their body. They will prefer to see the product on their hand. The problem is that the color of the skin on the hand is different from the color on the face. When I explain this to my clients, their second choice is the inside of their wrist. This is not the best choice either because this part of the body is probably the most protected from the sun. The truth is some women do not want to take their makeup off because they do not want me to see them.

Who am I? I am a stranger. It is never my intention to criticize or embarrass them. My job is to assist them with their skin care issues, help them look more attractive, and inspire them to feel their best.

One woman came in the other day looking for a specific product. When I showed it to her, I said, "Would you let me try some on you?"

"No, I don't want it on my face."

"That's fine. Let me show you by applying some to your hand."

"No, I don't want it on my hand, either."

In the end, I had to demonstrate the product on myself instead of on her. Self consciousness and fear of humiliation are the main reasons why some women will not allow me to see them without their makeup. Many of us respond the same way when we face God – shamed, fearful, and feeling inadequate. In Christ, we have God's unconditional acceptance. We are His sons and daughters, joint heirs with Jesus Christ. Our relationship with Him is not based on our contribution to Kingdom business. The level of intimacy we have with Him is in proportion to our understanding of His Lordship in our lives. As we walk with Him and submit to His will and ways, we start to behave out of a heart of love, just as He loves us. His righteousness in the earth is His way of doing things.

God is sitting and waiting, but He is not passive. He has done everything that He can do. He sent His Son, Jesus. There is nothing more that He can do for us. The Holy Spirit has been sent to prompt us to receive what has already been accomplished at Calvary. We have been given access to God through Christ. We have the forgiveness of our sins. He has imputed His righteousness to us. He promised He would give us an abundant life, which will come based on our level of intimacy with Him.

For example, when a woman comes to me looking for a foundation, but does not know what she wants, we are likely to spend half an hour together in my makeup chair to find the right foundation for her. Each of the different foundations has a different finish. Some are designed for dry skin, some for oily skin. Some foundations are designed for women who are minimalists and do not want a lot on their face. Some are heavier for women who want more coverage. No foundation is going to sit well on the skin unless I first clean the face, tone it, put a serum on it, and moisturize it. I have to create the canvas. If a client is unwilling to take off the makeup she was wearing when she came to the store, the makeup I try to put on over her makeup will never look the way it is supposed to look.

This is how you appear when you cover sin by pretending. When you have sin in your life, you have this residue, perhaps layers of residue that you try to cover up. You wear a mask and convince yourself that no one sees underneath. This is almost never true. In fact, it typically makes a bad situation worse. First, you need a cleansing. How do you do this? Well, you clean yourself through confession. After cleansing you rinse and tone yourself with water, which is the Word of God. Finally, you moisturize yourself with the oil of the Holy Spirit. This creates the canvas for your life.

Putting a cover over something that is impure will never benefit you. The practical application may be very simple, but you have to be willing to sit in the chair. You have to be willing to be cleansed, to be watered by the Word of God, and finally, to be anointed with the Holy Spirit. You have to be willing to submit to the treatment.

My treatment may be different from yours. God may have to use some strong word to discipline me and correct my behavior. This may require an astringent, something that has a bite to it. In your case, you may have already experienced a lot of astringents to correct issues in your life, leaving you sore. You need some heavy moisturizer, something soothing and cool. God is the ultimate makeup artist. He is the only one who is going to know which of those applications is right for you. He cannot get to you unless you come to Him. The Word says, *"Come to Me, all you who labor and are heavy-laden and overburdened, and I will cause you to rest"* (Matthew 11:28). You have to show up with God. The biggest part of success in Christian living is simply showing up and saying, "Lord, I'm here. I'm available. I'm willing. I'm listening." Then He begins to walk you through an individual prescription to heal you.

Some women come to my counter to return a very expensive skin care treatment. When I ask them what was wrong with the product, they say, "It didn't work." When I inquire further, they admit, "Well, I used it for a few days and I didn't see any results." These women do not understand that the damage to their skin is cumulative over many years. Repairing the damage will require an investment of time. They must be patient and consistently apply the product. It's the same with God. It may take time to heal your life and deal with the consequences of earlier behaviors. The Word says, *"Put your hope in the Lord. Travel steadily along His Path"* (NLT: Psalm 37:34). Spend time with God to find a new strategy for your life. Once you have done this, take the time to implement the strategy. Be consistent. There is no 30-day trial with God after which you can get your money back. Commit to a long-term relationship with God. He is not Santa Claus. He is the sovereign of the universe.

One of my favorite movies is *The Horse Whisperer* (2). In the film, a successful New York businesswoman is desperate to find healing for her daughter who was hit by a semi-truck while riding a horse on a wintery day. The horse lost its footing on slippery ice and slid into oncoming traffic. Tragically, the daughter's friend was killed instantly, though the daughter survived while losing her leg.

Her beautiful horse survived also, but is so damaged that it acts like a wild, crazy animal. Raging and out of control, the horse is no good to anyone. The vet recommends that the horse be put down. The mother decides that it would be too traumatic for her daughter if the vet shoots the horse. The daughter becomes angry, bitter, and terrified.

In an effort to heal them both, the mother drives with her daughter and the horse across country to Montana to a ranch owned by the character portrayed by Robert Redford. He is known as the Horse Whisperer. He has a reputation for healing horses. The mother hopes that healing the horse will help her daughter recover from her own emotional trauma.

At the ranch, the horse runs into an open field and will not let anyone go near it. The Horse Whisperer patiently and quietly sits a safe distance from the horse for hours at a time. Gradually the horse comes closer and closer, until it allows a human to stroke it. After enough time passes, it's time for the horse to be saddled and ridden, but it refuses to yield to the Horse Whisperer. Firmly and skillfully, he ties a rope around one leg in order to force the horse to kneel to the ground. It is brutal to watch. The Horse Whisperer has to hurt the horse in order to help it, but he isn't harming it. There is a difference. This is the only hope for the girl to be able to mount the horse on her own and ride. It is also the only way that the horse could fulfill its purpose once again. The horse has to kneel completely down. Both the girl and the horse have to have faith in the Horse Whisperer, even when it hurts.

There was a time in my life that when I felt like that horse. The devastation of my life was so great, and the damage was so severe it left me reeling. During this season, God sent precious friends into my life to be to me what the Horse Whisperer was to that horse. They did not push, or lecture, or fix, or condemn, or preach. For a long time, they were content just to be with me, warts and all. I clearly had outbursts of anger, self-pity, confusion, guilt, and a total loss of self-esteem.

It is amazing what the quiet, gentle spirit of a tender-hearted soul can do for someone who has been tormented and shattered. The Holy Spirit does indeed descend upon you as a dove when you become still. I will be forever grateful to those who saw my agony and allowed themselves to be used to bring me back to life and share their belief in God's purpose for me.

I am also thankful for the ones who came later. They helped me to see that the way to wholeness was not to cover over the hurt, but to deal with it and call it what it is. They helped me to face myself and my situation, while tenderly taking me by the hand to the only One who can do the necessary surgery.

Miss Martha tried to cover her growths with brown makeup. Other people try to cover over their pain with all sorts of addictions, including drugs, alcohol, work, money, sex, or fill in the blank. You just cannot put a band-aid on cancer and expect to be healed.

It takes a gentle, but expert surgeon. Some things just have to be removed. After that, it may take time in the intensive care unit. Then at some point you have to get up and live again. You have to learn to laugh again. You need to learn to walk away and leave the past behind. You need to be grateful for all you have and stop mourning all you have lost. There is a reason the windshield of your car is large and expansive, while your rearview mirror is small in comparison.

It may take a special friend to help you to know when it's time to heal and when it's time for you to reenter the race. Somehow you will make lemonade out of lemons. How do I know this? Because God cares about your redemption. I have personally experienced His redemption, and I am continuing to experience it now. Nothing is wasted. You may have to adjust, but you are alive for a reason. Scripture says, *"I call heaven and earth to witness this day against you that I have set before you life and death, the blessings and the curses; therefore choose life, that you and your descendants may live"* (Deuteronomy 30:19).

God is in your corner. You get to choose to life. No matter how badly it hurts or what you may have lost, you're still breathing. So for God's sake and the sake of all those who love you, yield to the Holy Spirit, kneel before Him and He will raise you UP!

Abba Father, I have been dealt a blow that I believed I would never be able to overcome. This is a lie. I can overcome anything because You have already overcome it for me. Pour in the oil and the wine of the Holy Spirit. Bathe me in Your presence. Send tender-hearted, spirit-filled companions to stand with me as I find my way back to You and Your purpose for my future. Like Job, help me to say by faith, "I know My Redeemer LIVES!" I don't know what tomorrow holds, but I know that You hold tomorrow.

Reveal to me what I need to see. Direct me when I need to move. Give me the courage to get up and go forward. I will live to declare the glory of the Lord!

In Jesus' name, so be it! Amen.

Makeup Lesson 8: Sunscreen

($) It's critical that everyone uses sunscreen. The sun is wonderful and meant to be enjoyed, but you must do so with caution. As we age, our skin frequently develops "age spots". The truth is many are actually sun spots. If you are seeing enlarged brown discolored spots on your hand or extremities, these can be a result of sun exposure. It is cumulative. If you see spots now, they are the result of exposure years ago. I recommend wearing a minimum SPF 15 and a maximum SPF 50. Anything over SPF 50 is unnecessary. Choose an SPF based on your amount of sun exposure.

Sunscreen should be reapplied every thirty minutes while engaging in outdoor activities. I believe products can be water-resistant, but not waterproof. You want to use products that specifically say "broadband sunscreen." This covers your exposure to UVA and UBA rays. You need to be protected from both. Pay special attention to coverage for your ears, nose, and lips where the skin is thinnest.

If you are fair-skinned with light eyes, it is critical that you pay attention to your sun exposure. If you burn your hand on a stove, your hand turns red and blisters. The same is true with sunburn. Your skin is injured and inflamed. Skin eruptions are nothing to fool around with or take lightly. If you are questioning a spot, and you are unsure, it is better to be safe than sorry. Melanoma is a cancer of the skin that you should take very seriously. See a physician who can prescribe advanced treatments. A cancer may be cured if caught early. Waiting can cost you your life.

Tanning beds are extremely dangerous. Avoid them. You can also receive sun damage from indirect sunlight, through car windows. If you are driving for hours in a car, use sunscreen on your hands and arms that are exposed. Pay close attention to bright sun reflecting off snow. I see a number of individuals over fifty coming in with environmental damage to the skin. That generation did not understand the risks of prolonged, unprotected sun exposure.

Lesson #9

No Greater Love

I was developing a very close relationship with my coworker, Diane. She worked for a different cosmetics line, which backed up to my bay. One Saturday she came over to me holding a business card in her hand.

"You are not going to believe what just happened to me!" she exclaimed as she flicked her hand toward me holding the business card.

"What?" I asked.

"A woman and her mother just came up to my counter looking for a specific color of lipstick that we carry. I looked all over for it, but couldn't find it. So I found one that was similar. I took the tester of the one she wanted and the tester of the one that was similar for her to compare. I drew a mark on my hand and showed her both colors. I said, 'See, this is almost the same shade. Do you think you might like this one?' Then she said to me, 'I don't know. I can't tell. I'm blind.'"

Diane continued, "Peggy, I was stunned. I started apologizing. I felt so foolish, but looking at her you would never have known that she was blind. She was looking straight in my face the whole time as though she could see me. I said to her, 'I'm so sorry.'

"Then she said to me, 'You don't have to apologize. My mother's here.'

"I turned to her mother, who took a good look at the two lipstick marks and told me, 'You know, I really…we just like our first choice. Why don't you look again? I've prayed about it. Please look one more time. I believe you'll find it.'

"So I said to her mother, 'Because you have prayed about it, I'll look again.' I went to look again and there in the drawer were three tubes of the lipstick the client wanted, bound together by a rubber band. I had overlooked them.

"As I turned around, I said to the women, 'Uh, well, here it is! Here's the color you want. I feel so embarrassed.'

"The blind woman replied to me, 'Don't feel embarrassed,' and she began to give me her testimony."

'I am very peaceful about my blindness, and very joyful. As a matter of fact, I have written three books, and I'm the CEO of two companies. I also have a syndicated radio talk show on 155 stations in 19 states and I'm a motivational speaker who travels internationally.'

"Then she explained, 'Years ago I had already given birth to my first child, and was pregnant with my second child in the first trimester, during which time I developed gestational diabetes. Suddenly, I started to hemorrhage behind my eyeballs.

'My doctor told me, "You really should not have this child. If you carry this baby to term, I can promise you that you will be blind for the rest of your life."

'I said to him, "Well then, there's no question about it. I will have this baby. If God wants to save my sight, He is capable of doing just that. I'm not going to abort this baby."

'My doctor responded by slapping his case file shut. He was furious with me when he told me I was making a foolish decision. I had my baby anyway, and since then I've been blind, just as the doctor predicted. I had three more children after that, five altogether. Now all my children are grown. My second child, the pregnancy that caused my blindness, is the one who has given us our three grandchildren. And now, my message when I speak to audiences around the world is how you can be a visionary. Being a visionary has nothing to do with having sight. Hope always sees and I am an ambassador of hope. People ask me, "How can you have so much joy when you can't see?" I respond by asking them, "How can you see and have no joy?"'"

"Peggy, I just stood there listening to this woman speak. Then she handed me her business card. I don't know why she did that."

"I do," I immediately replied. "She gave it to you because you were going to come over here and tell me this story. Now I'm going to contact her, because I want to invite her to be featured in my project."

It was very interesting to me that Susan Robinson, the woman played by Julia Roberts in the film, *Steel Magnolias*, also had diabetes. Susan also chose to have her child, and she died soon after giving birth. Diane's client chose to have her child and became blind. Both women chose life. The subsequent legacy of their choice was world changing.

Prior to this point in my relationship with Diane, I had never shared anything about my project, 'In Search of Steel Magnolias'. When I told her my plan, Diane was completely blown away for the second time that day. She eagerly volunteered to call the blind woman, whose name was Gail McWilliams. She told Gail a little bit about me over the phone and asked her if she would be willing to speak to me.

One week later, Gail walked into the department store with her husband, Tony. I took a break so we could go to a coffee shop in the mall. I began to share with them my testimony and my vision. Gail also gave me her testimony. I sat spellbound as she recalled her feelings of anger when she later had to come to terms with the consequence of her decision not to abort her baby. Her husband, always the spiritual leader for the family, told her, "We will not retreat!" She realized that no matter what, God was for her. Life wasn't for quitting. Gail was a prisoner of hope. To this day, she continues to keep her car keys in her purse.

Gail's blindness did not happen to just her. Her decision affected the rest of her husband's life, too. If she had aborted the baby, very few would have faulted her for it. Many people believe that a therapeutic abortion is the one exception to the rule when there might be a risk to the mother's life or health. Instead, Gail kept the baby, and then decided to have three more children, two daughters, and a son. With pride, she told me about the accomplishments and gifts of each child. Her miracle baby girls have grown into beautiful women who sing with her as she travels in ministry, just as I did with my parents.

As she was speaking, I noticed the tender and affectionate relationship she had with her husband. She gently reached out and touched him and asked him to get her hot water with lemon. He quietly acknowledged her and went to get it. As I observed his response to her, I realized that the makeup lesson for me that day was not only in her testimony, but also in the way this couple related to each other. He totally served her and appeared to be happy doing it. Tony didn't speak much during our meeting. He eventually took a walk and let us have a private conversation, not that I felt that we needed privacy. He genuinely seemed to love his wife.

Clearly I was witnessing the love of God, which created a spiritual bond between these two people. There was not a hint from him of bitterness or resentment or anything but love for the Lord, love for his daughters, and appreciation for his wife. I assume they experience challenges in their marriage as any other couple. Despite Gail's physical limitation, God allowed her to have a marriage partner and companion who would support her decision regardless of the consequences.

As Gail listened for an hour to my story and the vision that the Lord had given me, she was genuinely supportive and enthusiastic. I was amazed as I sat across from this woman who was completely content. She was one of the most joyful, peaceful, gracious, intuitive, and intelligent women I have ever met. She freely admitted that her blindness was a blessing. She could "see" the plan of God being fulfilled in her life. God gave her a platform to declare that she would not have kept her sight to lose her precious child. Each one of her five children has a ministry, and God is advancing Kingdom purpose through them. She speaks a lot for pro-life organizations for obvious reasons. It was a remarkable afternoon.

We finished and said goodbye. Walking back to the department, I thought about all the years of my life I felt as though I had been victimized. I was not discounting my own sorrow, hurt, or damage. In my personal journey, I had to grieve and put those issues behind me so that I could see my present opportunities. It was my choice when and how to do this. Joyce Meyer has recounted on her program, *Enjoying Everyday Life*, that when she was feeling sorry for herself she would cry out to the Lord, "Look what has happened to me!" I found the Lord's response to her to be compelling. "I know what happened to you. I also know that you have a *reason* to feel sorry for yourself, but not a *right*. I'm here to help you change it." I believe God weeps with us when we experience any loss or demonic attack. The good news is that we can be triumphant in Christ. There will always be a way out, around, over, through, or underneath. There will always be a way because Jesus is the way and He promised! We have to want Him. We have to believe Him. This is something no one can make us do, or do for us.

I found Gail to be a woman of strong character. She loved her family, and had a deep desire to live a powerful life with and for God. Her example challenged and motivated me to live the best life I can live. This gave me the answer I needed for that an inner, nagging voice questioning my decision to return to retail. *You're going backward. You have failed.* I have not failed! God is leading me in a new direction. The Scriptures say in Proverbs, *"The steps of a good man are directed and established by the Lord when He delights in His way and He busies Himself with His every step"* (Psalm 37:23). My steps are directed! This includes the stops and detours through my wilderness experience. The knots and pulled threads on the flip side of the tapestry, which look like mistakes to me, are part of the design that only God sees and reveals in His time. That is where we trust God blindly, just as Gail lives blindly, but confidently. There is no darkness with Him, only light. Jesus said, *"I am the Light of the world"* (John 8:12). I can learn to be as peaceful and content in the dark times of my life as Gail is in her life. I may not see clearly at times, but God sees my life and loves me. In every circumstance of my life, God is sovereign and in control. He is going to make good come from what is meant for evil.

I thought about how dramatically Gail's life changed the day she made her choice to keep her baby. I realized she could have also chosen to be bitter and resentful; to shake her fist in God's face and shout, "Why did You do this to me? How could You let this happen to me?"

Instead, this remarkable woman of faith has been able to turn the worst circumstance into her greatest blessing. God has used her life to show that joy does not depend on your situation. Happiness may be circumstantial, but joy is not. Joy is a condition of the heart and the soul. The Scriptures say, *"Be not grieved and depressed, for the joy of the Lord is your strength and stronghold"* (Nehemiah 8:10). He has elevated Gail and caused her to triumph by doing things through His power that she would never have done before. He has given her a global platform to show that anyone can overcome anything in life with the help of God.

The Lord ordered the steps of three righteous women the day that Gail came to purchase lipstick from Diane. God is clearly involved in everything, even when it looks as though He is not. For this I am truly grateful, particularly when I sometimes make the mistake of putting God and Satan on the same level. Often they may seem to me to be equal powers vying for my attention or control. Satan, though, is not equal to God. God is sovereign. Satan can only go so far, as we see in the book of Job. Satan said to God, *"Does Job fear God for nothing? … You have conferred prosperity and happiness upon him in the work of his hands, and his possessions have increased in the land. But put forth Your hand now and touch all that he has, and he will curse You to Your face"* (Job 1: 9-11). Satan's point was that Job serves God only because he is the richest man on earth with a beautiful wife and dutiful children. Of course Job is going to serve God! Despite the condemnation of his friends and remonstrations of his wife to curse God and die, Job chooses to continue being faithful to his loving God. In response to the many afflictions and suffering brought by Satan, Job affirms, *"I know my Redeemer and Vindicator lives"* (Job 19:25), and *"though He slay me, yet will I wait for and trust Him"* (Job 13:15). In the end, God honors Job's faithfulness and prayers for his friends by restoring his health, his family and his fortune twice as much as he had before (Job 42:10-16).

No matter what your challenge may be, it is your choice to say, "I'm still going to trust You, Father." Gail's choice was to keep her child and become blind for the rest of her life, or abort her child. Clearly this is a horrible position for any woman to be in, and I am certainly not condemning any woman who has had an abortion. Gail chose to be a mother raising incredible children, an author, an entrepreneur, and a spokesperson. Only when we get to heaven will we know how many people were touched not only by her life, but also by the lives of the children that never would have existed if she had chosen to save her eyesight. None of us know what is going to happen tomorrow, but each of us can choose how we respond to every situation we may face. We can either glorify God or we can curse God.

I recognize that I have been victimized in my own life not just by people and circumstances, but also by myself. I have been a victim of my own poor choices. I have been a victim of my lack of knowledge and failure to use wisdom. I have been sincere, but many times sincerely mistaken. Thank God He is bigger than all that. None of that defines me! I am defined by a loving parent who will not let me go and will hang in there with me until I reach the other side. Let the wind and the waves roar! God brings my life into balance.

While circumstances in this life may victimize you, you also have the choice not to live as a victim. You cannot change your past, but thank God that He has enough mercy, grace, and power to cover it.

The longer I live, the better I understand that every day I can make choices. Every day I can choose how I will perceive everything that has happened, or is happening in my life. I could, for example, resign myself to believing that my life is over. I'll never live again. I'll never love again. I'll never be fruitful again. I'll never… I'll never… Is that true or false? The truth is God is the source of all creativity. If I lose the ability to function in one capacity of my life, it does not mean that I have lost the ability to function in every capacity. Jesus died so that I can live a victorious life. God has an infinite number of ways He can use me.

There are probably gifts and talents within you which you have never explored. In Gail's case, she never knew that she would write books, give speeches, and run companies after she became blind. Surely she never anticipated that one day women would look up to her and say, "Wow! You are an inspiration!" You can live a full and complete life, and God can raise you up. He can turn any sorrow for your good and His Glory. That is what makes being a Christian so thrilling!

I left the meeting with Gail that day understanding that the entire encounter happened because of a tube of lipstick that Diane could not find. It could have just as easily happened that Gail would have asked for her preferred tube of lipstick and Diane would have found it right away. Then Gail would have made her purchase without giving her testimony to Diane and walked away. The whole conversation would have never happened.

Sometimes I wonder how people survive without Christ. Without the peace and salvation of Jesus, where do they go? How do they cope with the sorrows and tragedies of life? I went home that day encouraged, built up and edified. I realized that if Gail can live a joyful and fulfilling life which inspires people, then I can, too. And so can you. The same God that gives her power and strength to overcome has no less power and strength for you and me.

Abba Father, thank You for helping me to be triumphant over the unfathomable. You show Yourself strong on my behalf. You are an amazing God!

Lord, I am asking You to reveal Your presence to me and Your power within me to overcome all obstacles. You are the God for whom NOTHING is impossible. You capture every tear in a bottle. You are the healer of broken hearts and broken dreams. Show me the light at the end of the tunnel. Show me the rainbow in the clouds. Give me a renewed sense of purpose and destiny.

Surround me with encouraging friends and mentors who will show me how to rebuild my life and encourage me to make the choices You know are best for me. Do in my life what only You can do. Then You will give me beauty for ashes and the oil of joy for mourning. That is Your promise. I am counting on You!

In Jesus' name, so be it! Amen.

Makeup Lesson 9: Daytime Moisturizing

($$) Daytime Moisturizers may contain sunscreen or they may not. They may be in the form of a lotion or a cream. Lotions tend to be lighter and may be beneficial in the summer months. Creams are heavier and may be beneficial in the winter months. If you are normally very dry or normally oily, you may choose not to switch off seasonally.

Certain clients may have a reaction to sunscreen and may choose to purchase a product without that ingredient. If you do not have a negative reaction, it is my belief that everyone should be wearing sunscreen in some form or fashion. What's helpful is that you can achieve that protection within the context of your moisturizer. Sunscreens in moisturizers start out at SPF 15 and go up to SPF 50.

There are also tinted moisturizers that have sunscreen. You may use this instead of a foundation. This may be beneficial if you want some coverage, but you will be engaging in an outdoor activity, where you will be perspiring. You might not want any heavy makeup on in addition to the moisturizer as it would clog pores.

BB creams have become popular recently. This formula became well known in the Asian countries following laser surgeries. They are topical and provide treatment with some tint. BB creams can also be used as a primer under foundation. It gives a beautiful buildable finish as well as benefit to the skin, prior to additional steps. Even oily skin needs hydration. Your need for topical hydration may change based on your water consumption, your environment, and your physical activity.

Hormonal imbalances that change periodically as a result of age or pregnancy and menopause can cause changes in the need for hydration in your skin. You may need one moisturizer in winter and another in summer. If you are on certain drug therapies, this can increase your need for greater hydration. Typically as we age, the skin has a tendency to become thin and the need for moisture will be more of a concern.

Lesson #10

Circle Together

By now I had worked through three seasons - summer, fall, and winter. Easter was now approaching. Over time, I had gradually broken down barriers between some of my coworkers and me. As I got to know them, I understood how they were struggling in life. Several of the sales consultants working around me were single mothers. It seemed that every conversation reminded me of my experiences thirteen years ago when I was in a similar place. I remembered feeling the need to pray for my children continuously. I also remembered how much responsibility I had to shoulder by myself. It seemed as if every day presented a new challenge to overcome my fear and worry.

One night I was working with Diane. By nine o'clock, most customers were gone, but we were still open for another hour. I walked over to her.

"How has your night been?"

"Ugh! Hardly any sales tonight. It's hard to stand in one place when there are no customers. Now my feet are killing me. I'm ready to go home," Diane whimpered.

"I know. I'm ready, too. While we've got time, what shall we talk about? How are your daughters doing?"

"Oh, Peggy! I'm very concerned about my older daughter. She quit her job at a car dealership where she has been working for several years. She said she was miserable. She has a dream to complete her degree in fitness education, but she hasn't saved any money. She doesn't have a scholarship. She hasn't even applied to a school. I understand that she's struggling to find herself. I'm trying to help her, but my financial situation is tight. There's not much left after I pay my own bills.

"I'd like to see my daughters back in church and serving God. I cry out to Him to send them godly, Christian husbands who will love them and take care of them. There is only so much I can do to help them. Some of their choices seem so reckless to me. My younger daughter is really giving me fits. I feel as though I can't reach her. The other night I didn't know where she was. I didn't know when she would come home. I went into her bedroom and stretched myself across her bed and just wept before the Lord. The next day she came home and said to me, 'Mama, you were in my room last night. I can always tell because you leave your slippers at the foot of my bed.' She knows I'm praying for her."

I told Diane, "I understand your frustration and anxiety. Our battle for our children is vertical, not horizontal. We still love them as adults, but we are more effective when we express it passionately through prayer. I'm learning that God hears me when I pray, and He moves on their behalf. I just don't get to tell Him how or when to move. I have to be patient."

We don't wrestle with human beings, but with principalities and powers and rulers of wickedness in high places (Ephesians 6:12). God has given us mighty weapons for the pulling down of strongholds (2 Corinthians 10:4). We just have to pick up the right weapons and fight the right way. I have no access to two of my children. They live thousands of miles away. I used to cry myself to sleep some nights, sick with fear and worry, until I finally realized that God is not surprised by any of this. He is in a covenant relationship with us. What belongs to us also belongs to Him. He is completely aware of everything that involves them and He will be faithful to take care of what belongs to us.

When I shared this with Diane, she told me that she was in a leadership position in the prayer and counseling ministry at her church for more than ten years. I suggested that we should pray for each other and that we should stand in agreement with each other for our children. Diane agreed.

After the conversation, I felt compelled the next day to go to the bookstore to buy several copies of *The Circle Maker* (3), so that I could give them to Diane and another coworker with similar concerns about her children. The book talks about drawing a circle around specific promises that God has given us in His word regarding the challenges and obstacles in our lives. When I read this book, I found it to be very empowering.

As I listened to Diane's concerns, I quickly understood how frightened and overwhelmed she felt. I had no answers. There was nothing I could say to make anything better. I had my own Goliaths to kill. I decided the only thing I could do was to pray for her while I was praying for myself, and then give her some tools that I felt were helpful.

I gave her a copy of the book as an Easter present.

"What's this?", as she started to open the present.

"I hope you like it. It has meant a lot to me."

"*The Circle Maker.* Oh, Peggy, you are so sweet! Thank you!"

I am a very visual person. I cannot touch my children because they're so far away. It has helped me to take the scriptural principles in this book and turn it into a visual aid. The teaching is simple, yet profound. You draw a circle around the Jerichos in your life, which are situations, or strongholds, which seem impenetrable, and pray for specific results. You simply refuse to give up until you see the walls fall. This is spiritual warfare. It is not for the faint of heart. It requires a pit bull mentality to attack in a spiritual dimension and pray until something happens.

"After I read this book, Diane, I started a scrapbook. Here it is. This is where I keep pictures of my children. You see, and this is where I have written promises that I believe God has given me about them."

"Oh, that's wonderful!"

I continued, "I would also like to put pictures of your children in my scrapbook, so that when I pray for my children I will also remember to pray for your children."

"Would you?!", she looked at me with such gratitude.

"Yes."

"Well, I'll do that," Diane said, "but only if you'll give me pictures of your children with their names so that I can make my own scrapbook. You know, even though I was a prayer minister on the intercessory prayer team at my church for years, I have never seen anything like this. This is a great idea!"

"You know, Diane, it's late and there is no one here. Instead of waiting until we go home, why don't we just pray here, right now? We don't have to pray with our eyes closed. Anyone who sees us will just think that we're talking. Nobody will know the difference and we're not hurting anything. We both need miracles. We both need God to move on our behalf. What do you say?"

"I say yes. Of course! Why not?"

We agreed that night that whenever she would pray for her children, she would also pray for mine, and whenever I would pray for my children, I would pray for hers. We would stand together.

After that night, whenever Diane would see me come into work she would greet me sweetly with a hug. Then as closing time approached, and the customers went home, she would come over with this expression of glee on her face and whisper to me, "What are we going to pray for tonight?" This quickly became a habit that was so encouraging to both of us. Instead of standing around on our feet complaining about the lack of customers, Diane would share her scrapbook, and I would share mine. We soon realized that even though we were not making any commission sales, we were there to be a support system for each other. We were there to redeem that time by praying for our loved ones and each other.

One particular evening we were praying and crying out to God for our children. Diane's older daughter, the one who wanted to complete her degree in fitness education, was now making plans to go to California to be a "movie star". According to Diane, the daughter had no money saved, and no comprehension of both the cost of living in California, and the odds against her achieving her dream of becoming a full-time actress. At the same time, my daughter called me to say that she was having a great deal of trouble sleeping. I mentioned this to Diane. As we were standing there together, I prayed for her daughter while she prayed for mine. That night, I specifically prayed and asked God to speak to my children in dreams and visions, and Diane got into agreement with me.

> *Father, I lift up my children to You tonight. You know each of their needs. You know the longings of their hearts. I pray that You would send ministering, warring angels in the heavenly realm to do battle and to minister on their behalf. Protect them from the evil one. Give them wisdom and discernment. I cancel all satanic assignment against them. They will know the Truth and the Truth will set them free. I loose them from any and all relationships that would cause them to move away from their relationship with You and with me. Give them a tender heart toward You. Help them to hear Your voice and another's*

voice they will not follow. Speak to them in dreams and visions. Reveal Yourself to them in a unique and personal way. Heal their hearts. Show them Your purpose for their lives. Send them spouses that will love You and love them. Be unto them all that they need. Teach me how to cast the care of them onto You, knowing that You will be faithful to keep what I commit to You.

Thank You for forgiving me of my mistakes as a parent. You never stop parenting any of us. Your grace is sufficient to take up the slack for my human imperfections. May this time of prayer and intercession improve the empathy and understanding in my relationships. Thank You for hearing me.

I pray this in Jesus' name. Amen and so be it!

The following day, my daughter called me. "Mama, I want to tell you about something amazing. You know how I've always had trouble sleeping? Well, I came home from work last night. It was late, and I was completely exhausted. I collapsed across my bed and fell into such a deep sleep. I had an astonishing dream. I saw my hands and arms. Both arms were covered with bracelets from my wrists to my elbows. Each bracelet was made of beads - rows and rows of beads up my arms. Jesus was there. He showed me His big hands and muscular arms. He told me, 'Precious, do you see these beads on your arms? All these beads represent everything in your life that worries you. You are not meant to carry all those cares.' Then, one by one, He began to take the bracelets off my arm and slip them onto His arm. It looked really funny to me. He looked like a dad playing with His little daughter putting her bracelets on His big, masculine arm. I started laughing while He kept doing this until my arms were free, and all the bracelets were on His arms. Then He said, 'These were meant for Me so that your arms could be free.' I was in such a deep sleep, Mama. I don't know how long it's been since I slept so well. I woke up completely refreshed and totally at peace. And the first thought that came to my mind was that my mother must have been praying for me."

I said to her, "Well, Diane and I were praying for you last night. I prayed specifically that God would speak to you in dreams and visions. God is telling you that He is taking those things from you, but that doesn't mean that each day you live you won't have challenges or concerns. You have to get to a place where you can take those beads off and give them to God. He is willing to receive those things from you, but you have to take them off yourself and give them to Him."

I realized that God, again, in His sovereignty, had me working that night when I prayed with Diane. He ordained that Diane and I would be there together that night. We were learning not to panic over our children and keep all that pressure inside. We were learning the difference between venting about our children to each other and praying over them.

Prayer is the only expression that has the power to change anything. The Word of God also says, *"Again I tell you, if two of you on earth agree about whatever they may ask, it will come to pass and be done for them by My Father in heaven"* (Matthew 18:19). That's a promise! There is such power in agreement. When you are in agreement with another believer, someone who truly believes God, you can affect change.

There are endless opportunities for each of us to worry and get into fear. We can choose either to feed our fear or to feed our faith. It is like having a plug in your hand, and you have a choice between two sockets. You can either plug it into faith, or plug it into fear. Whichever socket you choose determines which current is going to run through you. Diane and I are making a conscious choice regarding our children. We know that there isn't anything we can do to stop, or fix, or change what is going on in their lives. After all, they are adults. So when we feel weak and frightened, we choose together to plug into faith. As a result, we are beginning to see God move and answer our prayers.

We used to stand around late at night and complain when there were no customers for us to make sales and commissions. Now we rejoiced because we chose to use that downtime to pray. God was redeeming our time.

The Word of God says, *"Be unceasing in prayer, praying perseveringly"* (1 Thessalonians 5:17). I don't think that means that you are to walk around constantly praying. I think it means that when an opportunity comes you don't wait, or say to someone, "Sure, I'll pray for you", intending to do it later when you get home, but never actually doing it. The concern is voiced; why not stop right there and pray? Pray immediately and consistently until you see breakthrough. When women who love God pray, it is remarkable to see how God moves.

Now when Diane and I see one another in between waiting on customers, we talk about the goodness of God. We praise Him for what He has done and what He continues to do in our lives. We talk about the miracles that we see.

One day after we had eaten our lunches on our break, I said, "We still have time on our break. Let's go outside and pray." We sat down, and Diane started to praise God. It was thrilling. Diane told me that her younger daughter had a wonderful new job that she loved. Even better, she had begun dating a young man who encouraged her to attend church with him. Diane was hopeful that this relationship was headed in the right direction. Also, her older daughter found employment in California almost immediately. She was rooming with responsible friends and had come home twice to visit.

Even when Diane and her daughters were not in agreement, the Lord was teaching Diane that He would never leave or forsake them. He cared about them, and He would cause everything in their lives to work together for good. Diane had been a single mother for eighteen years; her children were very small when she divorced. She was now learning, just like my daughter, to take those bracelets off and put them on the arms of God.

God is the only one who can do anything about such issues. The Word says, *"He is able to guard and keep that which has been entrusted to me and which I have committed to Him until that day"* (2 Timothy 1:12). He can handle it. He will honor His covenant with us.

It's very challenging to be a single mother. It's painful and terrifying to walk the floor in the middle of the night when you have a child, and you don't know where they are. There is no one next to you when you wake up; no one with whom you can share your heartache; no one to pray with you. You feel so alone, but God sees and cares. Scripture says, *"He will not allow your foot to slip or to be moved; He who keeps you will not slumber"* (Psalm 121:3). Sometimes I think the greatest work that God does is when we're sleeping. I wonder how much we impede the progress of God in situations and relationships because we will not give what is out of our control over to Him. We assume that this means we are giving up. There is a big difference between giving up on someone and giving them over to the only One who is capable of moving in them and for them. We cannot control the hearts or minds of people. We cannot stop people who are determined to misbehave. Sometimes we even lose that battle with ourselves. God, however, has an infinite number of ways to deal with me and those I love.

Diane and I frequently pray that God will bless our children, correct them, heal them, deliver them, confront them, love them, and discipline them. We pray the same for ourselves. *"God, do whatever it is that You need to do to draw us close to You, into a right relationship both with You and each other."* We would stand there and pray at work, then go home at the end of the shift feeling exhilarated. We would go home feeling assured that God heard us, and was working on our behalf.

It is very freeing and comforting to lay out all our concerns standing in agreement with each other, then release it to the Lord knowing that He is faithful. He is always faithful. He cannot deny Himself. He is going to accomplish His purpose. He is the perfect parent. He never stops parenting us, and He never stops parenting our children.

There are believers all around us. Do we ever consider that we could approach a coworker and say, "You know, I'm dealing with this issue. Would you pray with me about it at lunch?" I have done things here at my part-time job that I have never done in my life. I have to ask myself the question, "Why?" There is nothing super-spiritual or religious about what is happening. It's just people in conversation discovering that everyone has serious situations in life for which there are no easy answers. When I reflect on my life, I now realize after all these years that God is available every minute of every day. I can cry out to Him anytime I want, and He will hear me!

I once heard someone say if you are going to cry over something, then get into the habit of "crying *up*". Direct your tears and your voice up to God. If you don't have a prayer partner, ask God to highlight someone around you that will stand in agreement with you. Be careful. Use wisdom. I have been guilty of sharing too much information with individuals who never had my best interests at heart. It was a painful lesson in betrayal, but I refuse to be cynical. I understand that there are both genuine and counterfeit relationships. I have learned the hard lesson to be selective in choosing those with whom I am vulnerable.

I have a handful of beautiful Christian friends who have walked through fire with me. They are not perfect and neither am I. When life gets brutal we know how to "circle the wagons" as they did in the old west to protect themselves in battle. We cry *up* together. Our agenda is the cause of Christ and the benefit of those we love. As iron sharpens iron, we have the freedom to correct, exhort, admonish, and encourage one another, because we do not doubt the intentions or the love we have for each other.

The Word says, *"Confess to one another, therefore, your faults, your slips, your false steps, your offenses, your sins and pray also for one another, that you may be healed and restored to a spiritual tone of mind and heart"* (James 5:16). Many are afraid to do that because, unfortunately, some people are only interested in hearing the confession of someone's faults. Thus, our private hurts and agonies become fodder for gossip. So we learn to erect protective walls. We learn to hide from one another. We suffer in silence. That is not how believers were supposed to relate to each other. We are supposed to provide a safe place to land for wounded warriors, who are battle-fatigued in life.

When we isolate ourselves from others, we eliminate the possibility that we might learn from them. We become easy prey for an enemy who knows only too well that there is strength in numbers and danger in isolation. Why do you think Satan tries so hard to cause division in the body or in a family, or between a husband and wife? It is very simple. United we stand and divided we fall. It is not surprising that Satan uses the same tactics over and over again. He sets up circumstances that provide enough pressure to cause people to turn on each other. Unity must be important to God. That is why Jesus prayed, "*That they all may be one, just as You, Father, are in Me and I in You, that they also may be one in Us, so that the world may believe and be convinced that You have sent Me*" (John 17:21). In the upper room after Jesus was crucified, the disciples were instructed to go and wait. Scripture says, "*And when the day of Pentecost was fully come, they were all assembled together in one place, when suddenly there came a sound from heaven like the rushing of a violent tempest blast, and it filled the whole house in which they were sitting*" (Acts 2:1-2). It would be wonderful to see what God would do in our world today if everyone put aside their personal agendas to get right with Him and right with each other.

The situations Diane and I faced were very serious, and had the potential to be very emotionally draining. Because we chose to pray, God turned our makeup bay in the department store into an "upper room" experience. It became a holy place where God's presence was extraordinarily real and precious.

You may be facing challenges that you believe you cannot share with others. This is particularly true if the information involves someone else or they have asked you to respect their privacy. The great news is that Jesus can become your prayer partner. The Bible asks the question, "*Who is there to condemn us? Will Christ Jesus, who died, or rather who was raised from the dead, who is at the right hand of God actually pleading as He intercedes for us*" (Romans 8:34)? Isn't that a beautiful thought? Jesus is praying for me! When I don't have the words to pray, Jesus prays for me.

When you feel alone and overwhelmed, you can rest assured that Jesus is praying for you, too. When all else fails, you can ask the Holy Spirit to teach you how to pray over a particular situation. Sometimes the Holy Spirit will pray through you with a groaning that cannot be understood. Have you ever groaned before the Lord? Have you ever been so broken that there were simply no words to express your deepest emotions? Aren't you thankful that God knows you so intimately, that words are not necessary? He takes over to pray through you and for you.

People often behave in their own self-interest. They weigh you on the scale of assets versus liabilities. If you rank high on the asset side, they take your number. If you rank high on the liability scale, they take a hike. When God sees us high on the liability side, He runs toward us. We do not marvel that we would love Him but that He would ever love us. "*What is man that You are mindful of him*" (Psalm 8:4)? There is a lyric in an old song by Mike Payne and Ronny Hinson that says, "When He was on the cross, I was on His mind." Nails did not hold Jesus to the cross. Love constrained Him. Likewise, it is the love of God that constrains us. It holds us in relationship. The love of God brought Diane and me together in a fiercely loyal friendship.

Abba Father, please help me to love others the way You love me. Give me the heart of an intercessor. Help me to listen with a compassionate heart and stand prayerfully with them as they face the challenges of their lives. Help me never to be critical and judgmental. Remind me that I have never walked in their shoes. I don't know what brought about their circumstances. I have only a snapshot of their lives. You know their hearts. Give me wisdom and discernment.

Help me to speak only what You would have me to say. When words are inadequate or inappropriate, help me to listen intently and cover them with Your mercy and grace. Help me to be the kind of friend that will reflect Your Spirit. Teach me how to pray for others in every situation. I want to see the fruit of my prayers. Teach me to respect the confidences of people. Help me to come boldly before Your throne in unity, believing that I will see You answer me. Draw me close to You and to them.

In Jesus' name, so be it! Amen.

Makeup Lesson 10: Daytime Treatment

($$$) Many of the prestige lines carry specialty creams or lotions for daytime treatment of the skin. These products are designed to focus on specific areas of concern and individual issues needing repair or restoration. While some prestige line skin treatment products have been around for over one hundred years, the science of skin treatments is always advancing. I recommend working with a knowledgeable, experienced consultant who can analyze your skin issues properly in order to select the right product and set the right expectations for results.

Always understand what you are buying. Some daytime treatments are mixed with moisturizer products that may or may not also include sunscreen. Other treatments are not mixed with moisturizers. Using an issue-specific treatment requires an additional step in your daily regime.

Certain treatments will lift sagging skin and give it firmness. Other treatments will brighten the skin and add luminosity. Then there are specific treatments to address fine lines and wrinkles. The market has a variety from which to choose.

Women who suffer from Rosacea, manifested by acne or a fiery red color on the skin, or struggle with a sallow complexion, will benefit from treatments that smooth out the texture of the skin as well as neutralizing the variation of skin tone.

Finally, there are products on the market, which claim to provide solutions to multiple skin issues all in one step. Your trusted consultant can assist you in understanding how to meet your needs best without being redundant.

Daytime treatments will always be different from what is used at night. My customers frequently ask if they can use a daytime product in exchange for a nighttime product. My answer is no, because the consistency of the daytime product is always lighter, so that makeup may be applied after this step. Nighttime products are heavier. Also, you will not need sunscreen as you sleep.

Lesson #11

The Desire of Your Heart

I was working a full shift on Sunday. It was Mother's Day. Every year the fragrance department did a promotion where each client who purchased a fragrance set also received a beautiful, fresh orchid. Of course, the fragrance department was adjacent to the makeup bays. Both departments were decorated with Mother's Day signs. A live pianist was playing music. The store went all out to make the day a special event. In both departments, I witnessed the procession of people coming through to purchase a perfume or a makeup gift set to give to their mothers and wives to make them feel special.

For many years, I wished I could just go to sleep on Saturday evening the day before Mother's Day and wake up on Monday morning. I would have preferred to skip Mother's Day altogether. Instead, I would go to church with my husband. The greeters would offer small gifts to all the mothers and, of course, the pastor would ask all the mothers to stand. Attendance was usually higher from all the people who came into town that weekend to visit their mothers. Later, restaurants would be filled with families celebrating with their mother.

There was no celebration of me by my family. Year after year I went without so much as a card, or any other sort of acknowledgement from two of my children. Each Mother's Day hurt, until 2011 when everything shifted for me. I began to realize that God defined me. No man, no woman, no child defined me. Only Goes did. He saw my humanity, my faults, my weaknesses, but He also knew my strengths and the love I had for my family. He determined my value as a woman and my value as a mother.

These last three years, Mother's Day has not been hard for me at all as it has been in the past. Still, I noticed the trappings and hoopla surrounding the event at work. I could not get away from it.

One of the elements of Mother's Day is the giving and receiving of flowers. I love flowers. I love to get and give flowers. I remember my own mother, practical to her German bones, never saw the value of giving flowers that would be dead in a week. In my opinion, however, there is a message you send to a woman when you present her an extravagant gift of flowers. She is worth extravagance.

When I finally got to the place where lack of acknowledgment on Mother's Day didn't bother me anymore, because it no longer defined me, I could be joyful and happy knowing that God was with me. He understood me. He forgave me. He loved me in spite of myself. His reward is what I care about. How He sees me is what matters. Instead of letting myself become depressed, in my heart, I honored my mother, who had been my biggest fan. She sacrificed so much to help me follow my dreams. I spent my time, thanking God for having a Mom who taught me about Jesus. I was so fortunate to have been loved by my mother. I decided it would be her day.

It was amusing therefore, that this year on Mother's Day, God would find a very creative way to acknowledge me with flowers. At the end of the shift, my manager walked up to me with the last orchid plant in his hands. He put it on the counter in front of me, and said, "Happy Mother's Day!" and walked away.

Now he could have given that orchid to any of the other women working in the cosmetics and fragrance department that day. He did not give it, however, to just anyone. He gave it to me. My manager knew nothing about the hurt that I have felt on past Mother's Days. He knew nothing about the estrangement between my children and me. So why did he choose me?

Scripture teaches, *"Delight yourself also in the Lord, and He will give you the desires and secret petitions of your heart"* (Psalm 37:4). I realized that, in the last three years, I had begun to delight myself in the Lord. To my shock and amazement, despite my shortcomings, warts and all, I discovered that the Lord was delighted in me. When you delight yourself in the Lord, the Scripture does not say, "…and He will give you your basic needs." He does not give you food, shelter, or clothing in response to your delight. Instead, the Scripture says, "He will give you the *desires* of your heart."

I had never acknowledged that for all those years I really desired flowers on Mother's Day, as impractical as they may be. The true desire of my heart was affirmation and acknowledgment. It never occurred to me that I never felt that from the Lord until I delighted in Him. I always delighted in my children. I always delighted in my family. I even delighted in the creative visions and dreams I tried to accomplish in my career. It was not until I reached a point in my life where I felt as though I had lost everyone who had been around me that I realized what it meant to delight myself in the Lord. His unconditional love and affirmation exploded in my heart.

When you come to the end of yourself, even if it is a horrible place with no one around, you can look up and find that God promises that He will never leave nor forsake you. *"I will not in any way fail you nor give you up nor leave you without support. I will not, I will not, I will not in any degree leave you helpless nor forsake you! Assuredly not"* (Hebrews 13:5)! I wondered to myself, *Why did He say it this way? I will not, I will not, I will not.* Then, if you still did not get what He meant, He adds, "Assuredly not! I will never leave you. I will never forsake you. I will never relax my hold upon you." I remember when I read this I thought to myself how odd to write this with such repetition and emphasis. Once would have been sufficient.

Then I saw a picture in my mind's eye of a child in bed at night having a nightmare and crying out in fear. When a parent comes in knowing the child is frightened, she never says just one time, "It's okay." No, her instinct is to pick her child up into her arms and say, "It's all right. It's all right. It's all right. Mama's here. Mama's not going anywhere. I promise. I'm never going to leave you." I now understood that this verse in the Bible was translated as though God was speaking to a child who was scared to death.

God knows that there may be experiences in our lives which are not just bad, but absolutely terrifying. It may look as though the world has gone mad, no one is making any sense, and everything is crashing. God is there to scoop you up into His arms and say, "I'm never going to leave you. I'm never going to forsake you. I'm never going to relax my hold upon you. I promise. I will not. I will not. I will not. Assuredly not!" This is the same way a parent comforts a terrified child. That is what I experienced. God wrapped me up in His arms, and He loved me. He was delighting in me. And I was delighting in Him. I believe He orchestrated that love note to me on Mother's Day to say, "I see you as a mother. I know you. I know you are not perfect, but I am honoring you today. Even if the people whom you wish would honor you are not here, then I am going to make sure that somebody else is here to give you flowers so that you know it came from Me."

Often we may think that God doesn't care about us or our true desires, and we don't want to bother Him. We think God has His hands full with the universe and does not care about what I receive on Mother's day, whether it's roses or tulips, dark chocolate or white. God knows, though, how we are wired and what will make us smile and be happy. When my own children were growing up, it was never an effort for me to buy them a gift they wanted for their birthday. What parent doesn't get excited about creating a birthday party for a child, watching that child tear into that toy and jump up and down with glee and excitement?

Why do we not perceive God as gracious and attentive? Our relationship with God depends on how we see Him, and how we understand His character. Who is He? What is He like? Max Lucado wrote a wonderful book called, *The Applause of Heaven* (4). This book revolutionized my life and my understanding of the nature of God. The premise of the book is that when I roll out of bed in the morning, despite my morning breath, disheveled hair, and need for a shower, God is excited to see me and He says, "Oh, look! She's up! That's my daughter. Isn't she gorgeous? Just look at her!" God applauds me when my feet hit the floor in the morning. I do not have to accomplish anything great to earn His love. I just have to be me. Very much like my own child. As soon as my baby wakes up in the morning, I scoop him up, nasty diaper and all, and hug and kiss him. I can't wait to see my baby. I can't wait to hold him. I think he is the most beautiful baby ever, because he is mine. That's how God feels about me.

If we embraced the fact that this is how God feels about each of us, would it be hard for any of us to want to be in relationship with Him? Would we think that He was out to hurt us? Would we think that He was up in some boardroom making decisions about whether we pass or fail? God is nothing like that. God is "Abba", which means "Daddy". As adults, who prays by saying, "Dear Daddy, would you please help me?" That sounds ridiculous to pray that way, yet the word that He wants us to use when we relate to Him in prayer *is* "Abba". Who prays like that?

When I was little, and my father would introduce me to others, whether to one person or to the entire congregation, he would say, "This is my treasure, my precious Peggy Lee." If my earthly father could love me that much, then how much more would my heavenly Father love me? I don't have to worry as I go through the mundane routine of life that I cannot go to God because He is not going to be impressed with me. I am unique. He has a plan and purpose for my life that he formed before the foundations of the world. He knows my past, present, and future.

When I think about God in that context, then it is not surprising at all to think of God saying, "I know Peggy is lonely. I know she is feeling unappreciated as a mother. I also know she likes flowers. I know she needs affirmation and acknowledgment. Because she has been about my business, I am not only going to meet her needs, I am going to give her the desire of her heart because she pleases Me. I am going to see to it that she gets flowers on Mother's Day."

Some people would look at flowers from my manager and call it a coincidence. If you believe that God wants to show you how much He loves you, however, He will send you love notes. A love note is a remarkable, unusual circumstance or unexpected gift which is so significant to you, that you know it comes from Him. God desires to have a divine romance with you. He sends flowers. He chooses blush colors. Yes, He does. He is that gracious and attentive. He is the ultimate lover. Most people have a hard time with the concept of God being in love with us. He certainly had to be in love with us in order to send His only Son, Jesus, to give the ultimate sacrifice for our salvation.

God wants to have an intimate relationship with you. Perhaps you don't think you deserve that kind of relationship with Him. Perhaps you think that God is still some unreachable, ethereal being. Perhaps flowers are not the desire of your heart, but God knows the desire of your heart, and He is absolutely that nice!

Dear Daddy, thank You for being such a gentleman. Thank You for being ever mindful of me. Thank You for being tender and thoughtful. The world can be such an unkind and brutal place. I am asking You to send me a love note, something unique and very personal that You know I would enjoy. Help me to look to You as my source recognizing that people, even the best of them, will sometimes disappoint me. We are human beings. You are the faithful lover of my soul. You never disappoint me. You do only what is in my best interest. Restore to me a sense of my femininity. Restore to me a sense of my value to You. Help me to understand that You are the only One who defines me.

Whatever You choose to give, I ask that You clearly show me that it comes from You. Teach me to expect spontaneous acts of love and kindness from You. As I grow in this expectation, help me to be alert to opportunities You set up for me to be used as Your love note to someone else. I know that I cannot give away what I have never had. I will no longer let my well dry up as I give water to others.

You are always available to give water to the thirstiest of souls. You never run dry. Fill me up with your Holy Spirit until I am no longer thirsty and am running over.

I know You will do this for me because I ask it in Jesus' name. So be it! Amen.

Makeup Lesson 11: Nighttime Moisturizing

($$) Sleep is one of the best gifts you can give yourself for many reasons, including proper care of your skin. Your body repairs itself while you sleep. The skin is the last part of the body to repair in the sleep cycle. Loss of sleep clearly affects the appearance of your skin. This is true particularly around the eyes where the skin is more fragile.

The ingredients in nighttime skin care will always be richer and more concentrated. It is critical that no matter how tired you may be, you should never sleep in your makeup. The steps for proper skincare are easily learned, and the routine at night does not have to take long at all. Ask your consultant to help you become proficient with the steps. For every night that you do not remove your makeup and treat your skin appropriately, you will look as though you have aged seven days.

Start with the critical step of removing the dirt and makeup from the surface of the skin. Then tone and add your eye treatment and serum. Finally, use a moisturizer that is specifically tailored to your needs.

Aging is primarily the result of cell damage due to free radicals, pollution, and lifestyle. Nighttime products will renew your skin by adding moisture along with a dose of anti-oxidants. Some products claim to assist in repairing damage done to the skin on a cellular level. Other products are combined with creams that address specific concerns such as fine lines, wrinkles, loss of firmness, and elasticity. These products are designed to work in conjunction with a daytime regimen.

If you have a moisturizer that is too rich for you, it may cause you to break out. Do not omit this step. Just find the product that best suits you. The need for nighttime moisturizer is particularly critical as you factor in your daytime exposure to the elements. If your job or daytime routine causes you to be outdoors, make your nighttime regimen a priority so that your body can repair the skin while you sleep.

Lesson #12

Guard Your Peace

Anastasia was having difficulty keeping her patience. This was her third difficult client in the last two hours.

"Look at this dress. It's labeled a size 10."

"Yes, ma'am," Anastasia patiently confirmed.

"I wear a size 8. This dress is clearly mislabeled. It's way too tight on me. Don't you have another dress in this style that's a size 8?"

"Let's take a look, ma'am." Anastasia started to walk from behind the counter over to the racks when the other sales consultant came over.

"Anastasia! I'll help this customer," the sales consultant said rudely. "You were supposed to clear the fitting rooms earlier. It has to be done before you leave tonight. Go do it now!" It was already 6:00 p.m. There was a small staff at work that night. She thought of how exhausted she would be when she finally got home.

"Okay, just a minute." Anastasia had just about reached her limit. She would have finished clearing the fitting rooms two hours ago except her manager called her to the floor during the afternoon rush. Instead of doing what she was told, she headed toward the bathrooms and said, "Right away, as soon as I take a quick break." As soon as she was out of sight, Anastasia detoured to the escalator and headed to the first floor. At the bottom of the escalator were the makeup and jewelry departments. She darted back and forth between departments. She would pick up display items, or lean over cases of jewelry. Although she seemed to be looking for something, she never paid attention to what she was seeing. Her mind was racing with random thoughts generated by her frustration. How much longer could she put up with this mean coworker? Should she try to find a different job?

I was working that night and was about to start my closing duties when I noticed Anastasia, who is a small, frail woman. She appeared anxious for some reason, so I approached her. I took a quick peek at her name tag and said, "Hello. I see that you work here, uh… Anastasia. That's a pretty name. It seems you're trying to find something. May I help you?"

"Oh! No. Thank you. The truth is I'm hiding out here for a few minutes. I had to come down here to calm down. My coworker is just mean, and she makes me upset all the time. I get so upset I can't even think straight. On top of that, I've had some very difficult customers today. They seem to think I can't do anything right. Do you ever have customers like that? I'm just having one of those days. Sometimes I think these people will drive me crazy. I get so upset that I can't eat. It makes my stomach hurt." Half whispering, she told me the events that sent her scurrying for a safe place to hide.

"I'm sorry," I said empathetically. Rather than try to answer Anastasia's question, I searched for a way to change the subject. "You know, your English is so good and you have a beautiful accent. Where are you from?"

"I'm originally from Russia. I grew up in Leningrad, but now it's called St. Petersburg. Have you ever been to Russia?"

I could hear the tone of Anastasia's voice lift immediately. "No, I haven't, but my husband has. He says St. Petersburg is a beautiful city. Isn't it also called the 'Venice of the north'?"

"YES! That's right." Now Anastasia was excited. "Oh, how I loved growing up there. The art at the Hermitage is incredible, and the Peterhof gardens are so beautiful in summer. You know, I loved so much to go to the ballet and theater with my parents. Do you know Bolshoi ballet? Bolshoi means 'big' in Russian. I dreamed of dancing in the Bolshoi in Moscow, but instead I got married and moved to Amsterdam with my husband."

"Really! How long have you and your husband lived in Dallas now?" I tried to keep the conversation moving in a positive direction.

"My husband didn't come with me to America. We're divorced. He lives in Holland with my daughter. I came here with my son. It's hard. I don't get to see my daughter very often. I miss her." Without hesitating, she took out her cell phone to show me pictures of her beautiful children.

Moments later I could see Anastasia's expression change from delight back to sadness and dejection. I didn't need any more details. I understood the circumstances and could relate to Anastasia's feelings of separation. Anastasia was a foreigner away from her native country. How much latent suspicion does she still encounter as a Russian in America? On top of that, she was a single mother raising one child while separated from the other. That's a life that could make any woman fearful, anxious, and lonely.

"I'm sure you do," I assured. I know how you feel. I have a son and daughter living in Miami with their father. He and I divorced when they were in their early teens. They're adults now, but I don't ever get to see them. I also have an older daughter, my first child. She lives here in Dallas."

Anastasia was starting to relax again. "Peggy, you seem so peaceful. How come you're like this? How is it that customers don't bother you? You don't see your children either, yet you have such peace."

Anastasia had no idea that just that very morning I had learned that my daughter living in Miami had boarded a plane to go to London by herself, supposedly to work for some Saudi businessman. It sounded highly suspicious and dangerous. Of course, I was alarmed and frustrated because I had no input in the decision. I considered not even coming to work that day. Up until the moment I met Anastasia, I had been walking around in a fog considering various scenarios for my daughter's future. How bad could it be? I had no idea that in the middle of my own crisis I would have the opportunity to minister to Anastasia.

I told Anastasia that I had an experience a few years back, which almost cost me my life. It changed me in so many ways. One of the ways it changed me was that I realized how much of my life I wasted working myself into a knot about things over which I have no control. On top of that, I stopped reacting to people's bad behaviors. I have learned that when customers were irate or impatient, the majority of the time it had nothing to do with me at all; they were struggling with something else. There were a number of different ways I could respond to people like this. I didn't have to get drawn into their drama or solve everyone's problems. I realized there was only one Jesus, and I was not Him. When I finally figured that out and got over my messiah complex, I became surprisingly lighthearted and free.

I went on to tell her that life is full of serious issues like disease, death, and divorce, but some people waste too much time worrying about the trivial. My mama used to have an expression that I always thought was so funny. She would tell me, "Well, they can get glad in the same pants they got mad in." As I understood her, this didn't mean I should go around with a chip on my shoulder. I just became protective of my peace. Where there is peace, there is power. This was so important because I have lost my peace plenty of times in my life. When I lose my peace, I lose my ability to hear the voice of God, and to understand how He wants me to respond to a situation.

Who knew this would be such a revelation to me? There have been many times in my life where I have been in trouble because I was pushed emotionally, or backed into a corner. When my world was caving in, I reacted, and almost every reaction was wrong. I hadn't thought about it. I hadn't prayed about it. I didn't know what God thought about it.

So many of the negative consequences I have experienced by reacting this way I might have avoided if I had taken a moment to breathe. I could just breathe, calm down, and seek God. He would give me an answer because He said in His Word that, "*...He is the rewarder of those who earnestly and diligently seek Him*" (Hebrews 11:6). The Word also says, "*If any of you is deficient in wisdom, let him ask of the giving God who gives to everyone liberally and ungrudgingly, without reproaching or faultfinding, and it will be given him. Only it must be in faith that he asks with no wavering, no hesitating, no doubting. For the one who wavers is like the billowing surge out at sea that is blown hither and thither and tossed by the wind*" (James 1:5-6).

"Anastasia, God is not up there playing a childhood game of 'Guess what I've got in my hand,'" I told her. "He's more eager for us to be in the center of His will than we are to be in it. If you ask for direction and guidance, He'll give it to you, but you have to be willing to do what He says when He answers you. You may not hear the voice of God because you don't believe He would speak to you. Perhaps you have been running from Him or avoiding Him. You may not be hearing His voice because you're afraid of Him, afraid of yourself, or afraid of what He will ask you to do. If that's the problem, then you don't understand that God adores you. He is absolutely over the moon about you. Scripture says, '*...the Lord bestows grace and favor and glory! No good thing will He withhold from those who walk uprightly*' (Psalm 84:11). Why would a loving father ever withhold anything good from you?"

You may be praying about God meeting a financial need in your life and He may answer you by telling you that He wants you to forgive someone who has hurt you. One thing may have nothing to do with the other; God's perspective is totally different from ours. We want to address the outside issues, as women do, by nipping and tucking, primping, curling, and dieting. God wants to give you an inner beauty of the soul. He is concerned with the fruit of the spirit, which includes love, gentleness, meekness, joy, kindness, patience, goodness, longsuffering and self-control.

These things are not mutually exclusive. Be beautiful. Take care of yourself. Honor the body God has given you. Thank Him for every positive attribute about yourself, but keep it in perspective. We will age. Gravity will take its course. Wrinkles and gray hair will come. Our spirit, however, will live forever.

God says if you are struggling for an answer, or you are losing your peace, you can ask Him and He will give you an answer. He'll give you a way out. He'll show you the means. He'll reveal truth to you.

When we get pressed in emotional situations, or people push our buttons, typically the last thing we do is stop. We do not understand the power of stillness. There is such power in being quiet and waiting for God to give you direction. Sometimes He wants you to do something, and sometimes He wants you to do nothing. You've heard the expression, "Don't just stand there, do something!" Well, with God, He frequently wants to tell you, "Don't just do something, stand there!" You have to know when it's time to do something, and when it's time for you to sit down and shut up because God wants to do something.

In the sequel to *The Princess Diaries* (5), a Disney movie starring Anne Hathaway and Julie Andrews. The granddaughter, played by Anne Hathaway, is a "princess in training" to the Queen of Genovia, played by Julie Andrews. The young girl had been behaving in a way that was beneath her and apologizes to the Queen. She says, "I'm sorry Grandma, I guess I just lost it." The Queen responds by saying, "People like us don't get to lose it. We are the ones who are supposed to have found it."

Scripture teaches us that as believers, we "*...are a chosen race, a royal priesthood, a dedicated nation, God's own purchased, special people, that [we] may set forth the wonderful deeds and display the virtues and perfections of Him who called [us] out of darkness into His marvelous light*" (1 Peter 2:9). We are ambassadors of another Kingdom. From time to time, we all have acted as though we just "lost it". The difference is we have not lost the love of God. We have not lost His desire to see us fulfill His divine destiny for us. As I have frequently told my daughter, if you take one step toward God, then He will take ten steps toward you.

If you feel as though you've lost it, the good news of the gospel is that all you have to do is turn around and run back into God's arms. You will run right into His grace. On the other hand, as part of the royal priesthood, it may be time for you to grow up in Christ and start displaying the "manners of the court". It may be time to put away childish things. It may be time to realize who you are in Him and that the world is watching you. If the world cannot hear what you say as a Christian, it may be because people are too busy watching what you do. No human being is perfect. You really do have an adversary who sets you up for failure. You also have a God who is greater and who has given you a way to escape from every temptation (1 Corinthians 10:13), including the temptation to worry. Worry as a sin which claims that God is not sufficient to be all that we need.

"You have no way of knowing this, Anastasia," I continued, "but just today I found out some news about my daughter in Miami that is causing me to be very concerned. There was a time in my life when I would have been a complete wreck over this, chewing on my nails and totally hysterical with fear. Instead, I'm working today, and I've made up my mind that I'm throwing the care for my daughter's safety and well-being onto God. He loves my daughter more than I do. After all, He died for her. I suppose this is why you're looking at me and asking me why I'm so peaceful. This is what the Bible refers to as *'peace which transcends all understanding'* (Philippians 4:7). I could be a complete wreck emotionally, but I'm not. It's all about choice, Anastasia. I have chosen how I'm going to respond.

"I used to live a life of quiet desperation, and sometimes it wasn't so quiet. It was more like screaming desperation. In my mind, I saw my house burning to the ground, and all the people that I loved were sitting in rocking chairs on the front porch while I was screaming at the top of my lungs. We were in dangerous, life-threatening situations, and they just kept rocking away.

"While they continued to rock, I continued to scream as the house and my family, metaphorically speaking, went up in flames. My panic attacks and desperate pleading and crying changed nothing. It simply alienated the ones I loved from me, and made me physically sick. My focus was perpetually outward. I failed to look inward at my own unresolved pain and agony. I was a twisted, angry mess. It was not until a few years ago that I understood that when a circumstance or someone I love threatens to knock me flat on my back, I was supposed to get down on my knees in prayer and fight like a man."

I explained to her that I can't make anybody do anything they don't want to do. I can't convince anybody to see what they can't or won't see. People will see what they want to see when they are ready to see it, myself included. God does not force us to love Him or serve Him. Sometimes He will give us exactly what we were determined to get, because He knows that the painful consequence of our disobedience will lead us right back to Him.

On the surface, when God gets involved in relationships it may appear that things are going from bad to worse to ridiculous. Sometimes things have to fall apart completely so that God can put them back together. He is the master builder. That is why the Scriptures teach us, *"Except the Lord builds the house, they labor in vain that build it"* (Psalm 127:1). God has to build, and sometimes completely rebuild relationships from the foundation up. He has to send in the wrecking crew first. Anybody who has ever tried to live in a house that's being remodeled understands what a painful, messy process this can be.

I have chosen not to give up my peace. I try to avoid allowing anyone to tie me into a knot so that I cannot sleep, eat, or think. I now recognize that the peace of God is my spiritual birthright. It is always my choice to give it up. Jesus said, *"Peace I leave with you...Do not let your hearts be troubled, neither let them be afraid"* (John 14:27). The world did not give peace to me so the world cannot take it from me. I have to relinquish it. We all have that ability to choose our responses to every circumstance. We even get to choose Jesus, or not. He gives us the opportunity to choose Him or to reject Him.

When I finished ministering to Anastasia, she expressed her gratitude and told me she felt better. Smiling, I told her, "Giving yourself stomach problems because you are anxious will not change your situation one bit. There is One I know who can touch your life, change your circumstances, or give you the grace to overcome. I'll be praying for you."

Anastasia hugged me tightly and walked away smiling. The peace of God is infectious and transferrable. It is tangible; you can feel it.

Since that encounter, I would see Anastasia from time to time at work. She would always wave with a smile on her face and then come up and give me a hug. I started to notice this kind of reaction from the other coworkers with whom I had been able to share a similar moment. I guess you could say that I chose to be empathetic and vulnerable with my own humanity and then directed them to the Source of all power. It has occurred to me that Jesus instructed us to go out and "be" witnesses. He didn't say go out and "do" witnessing (Acts 1:8). I believe that many people in the world are broken and desperate for answers. I am not so sure that they are the slightest bit impressed with the way I debate God theologically. I am completely sure that they are very observant of the way I walk out my own struggles and issues, which speaks volumes. People can debate my theological position, but they cannot refute my personal experience. My effectiveness as a witness depends on my testimony about my personal experience and knowledge.

I was not "doing" very much. It was just that my presence would make my coworkers smile and remind them that they were not alone. I cared. God cared. There's a famous hymn called "What a Friend We Have in Jesus". My mother said she heard a man say once, "Don't sing to me about what a friend I have in Jesus, until you can show me what a friend I have in you."

I am realizing that the peace, love, and acceptance of God are powerfully appealing to people. I do not have to stand on a corner thumping a Bible. I do not have to preach to people. All I have to do is be the love of Jesus in the world. Offer an encouraging word. Care for people. Listen to their concerns. Pray for them. Each encounter does not necessarily need to lead to some sort of spiritual experience at a particular time where someone finally receives salvation. Sometimes I will plant. Sometimes I will water. God will provide the increase. He uses me to start a work in specific people who have not accepted Him, and one may never know what that work is or where it will lead. That is His business.

I never know how much my smile, encouragement, compliment, or affectionate pat on the back will impact a person. It could be like spoon-feeding water to a weary traveler falling over in the desert. Some people are that dry, that hungry, or that lonely and desperate for a touch from God. I want to be the hands, the feet, the love and the expression of Christ on earth. I pray that He uses me this way.

An example of this occurred several months later when I was doing a book review for my Bible study group on a book entitled, *The Secret Holocaust Diaries* (6). This book is a biography of a woman named Nonna Bannister, who began life as the daughter of a Russian aristocrat. She and her family suffered gruesome atrocities and witnessed executions during the Bolshevik Revolution.

She and her mother were the sole survivors of the family, but survived only to be imprisoned by the Nazis during World War II. Of her entire family, Nonna was the only survivor from Hitler's concentration camp. At age 19, she emigrated to Louisiana under the sponsorship of an American Baptist church. Her unwavering faith in God gave her the supernatural ability to live a life of grace and forgiveness for fifty-two years, without anyone knowing the truth about her past, including her husband and children. They never suffered any residual effects of the unspeakable agony which she endured. She walked that out with her Savior, just the two of them. She was committed to living a life that would benefit those around her, filled with joy and purpose, and dedicated to those she loved who were brutally murdered during the war. Only God can do that in the life of a human being.

I was struggling with the preparation of the book review because I couldn't pronounce the names of the Russian characters very well. I heard Anastasia's voice one day at work when it dawned on me that she could help me. "Anastasia! I'm doing this book review about a woman from Russia." She enthusiastically agreed to teach me how to pronounce not only the characters' names, but also the names of the towns and cities mentioned in the book. She even gave me the name of a local bakery so that I could bring native Russian baked goods for people to sample the night of the book review. Anastasia was so excited that I took an interest in her country. She was intimately familiar with her country's history and the genocide that was inflicted upon the Russian people during that period. While she revealed no details of her past to me, I could tell that she was wrestling with some painful issues. Asking for her assistance with my project gave me an opportunity to talk about the grace of God, which can heal our wounds, and free us from bitterness, resentment, and hatred. I believe that, through me, God was affirming her value and recognizing her worth. I was able to communicate to her that there is hope in Christ to overcome the worst that human beings can do to one another.

How about you? Are you struggling with something or someone that you feel is unforgivable? Are you unable to forgive yourself?

Forgiveness is a process which leads to healing and restoration. The greater the perceived damage, the more time you may need to recover emotionally, mentally, and spiritually. God can give you an instantaneous healing, but deep wounds understandably require more than a minute.

When I truly lay down my pride and confront my own humanity, I see others more easily through the eyes of God. In my life, the hardest person for me to forgive is myself. I cannot turn back time, or unsay words I have said, or undo some things that I have done. Neither can anyone else. Even God does not change the past. My mother used to say, "You can't unscramble eggs!" With respect to my mother's amusing wisdom, God can make some terrific omelets. He is the only one who can restore to me the years that the locust has eaten (Joel 2:25). God wants to heal my broken heart. He has the means to accomplish emotional and spiritual restoration. Ultimately, it is His work to complete. I just need to show up and be willing to exchange His beauty for my ashes.

Dear Daddy, life can be excruciating. I wonder how I will ever recover from wounds that I have suffered from the selfish, inconsiderate behavior of others. Have I also behaved the same way toward them? I am afraid that if I start peeling away at the many layers of agony to get to the bottom, I won't survive it. This is the perfect environment for bitterness, resentment, and hatred to flourish. I resolve that, by Your grace, I will not allow these strongholds to take over my life.

Daddy, you see my deepest wounds. Cover them with Your mercy and grace. At the same time, I know that I have responsibility for my own healing. I am also Your minister of reconciliation in the earth. It is Your desire that all would be reconciled to You and that we would be reconciled to each other. Give me faith to believe that no matter what the transgression, You are more than able to accomplish the necessary work in my heart and in the hearts of those I love as well.

Help me to pray for my enemies who have inflicted upon me damage or loss for which I will never be compensated in this life. Help me to understand that You will balance the books. You are the Righteous Judge. There will be a day of justice and recompense.

While I recover, restore to me the joy of my salvation, which is my strength. Show me the path to wholeness. Fill me with Your love.

In Jesus' name, so be it! Amen.

Makeup Lesson 12: Body Skin Care

($) An appropriate skincare regimen for the body is no less important than it is for the face. People have a tendency to focus only on that which the rest of the world sees and neglect the rest. Just as there are appropriate cleansers, exfoliants, moisturizers, and treatments for the face, there are products to treat the elbows, knees, and feet, as well as everything else.

There are particular prestige lines that have advanced products that will assist with stubborn cellulite. They contain natural, plant-based oils often used in massages. Some contain fragrances while others are fragrance free. Other products focus on the nail beds and the cuticle area of the hands. Still other products revitalize and moisturize the feet, and assist in the treatment and elimination of calluses. Calluses are a frequent issue for clients who spend a great deal of time on their feet. They can be painful and may also require a pedicure for relief. In this case, proper care of the skin on your feet may reduce the frequency of pedicures needed.

Hydration for the skin is important all over the body. You may see a need for more moisture based on the same lifestyle issues previously addressed. If you are exposed to the elements regularly, or if you are taking medications, or if you have a light complexion with a tendency toward thin skin, you will need more moisture. Cold climates will also dry out the skin.

The best way to use moisturizers on the body is to use them right after a hot shower while the skin is still moist and a bit damp. If your body lotion has a fragrance, this can be the first layer of fragrance as you make yourself up. I recommend using a body shower gel which has extra emollients, rather than soap which tends to dry. Some of the prestige lines have exfoliants that will slough off the dry skin on the body. These should be used carefully as they might tend to dry your skin if used too frequently. I suggest you use exfoliants twice weekly, the same way you would exfoliate the face. Certain oils will refresh for the morning and others will have components that cause the body to relax after a hard day. A nice bath not only cleanses the body, it also relaxes the muscles. In certain cultures, bathing is considered a treatment for the body and the soul.

Lesson #13

Love Who You Are

One evening I was working at a bay for a cosmetics line different from the one which I normally manage, when an attractive looking lady who appeared to be from the Middle East came up to my counter. She immediately grabbed my attention.

"Excuse me! I know I look terrible. Can you help me?" She had a desperate tone in her voice. "I have these bags under my eyes. See these dark circles? Can you help me find something to cover them up or make them go away?"

Women will often come to my counter and start apologizing for the way they look. I think it may have something to do with the fact that image is important in selling cosmetics. The consultants, therefore, are always well made up. Our job is to represent our product lines well. Consequently, when women come in to shop, not necessarily looking their best, they see a consultant and feel compelled to give an unsolicited explanation for their appearance.

"Why don't you have a seat and let me take a look," I replied.

She continued, clearly distressed. "I haven't been sleeping. I was in a car accident earlier this week. I have been very upset. I was rear-ended. The driver of the other car was clearly at fault, but the truth is I was returning from a custody hearing for my son. I could not believe that the judge gave custody to my Egyptian ex-husband."

In the course of about five minutes, this woman gave me the highlights of her life story in order to explain why she was looking so harried. She was only about twenty-five or twenty-six years old. She was not Egyptian, but explained to me that she was from Persia, or Iran.

"Look at this!" She pulled out her cell phone to show me a picture of the damage done to her car. "Thank God I have insurance! But this is Dallas, you know! Who can get around without a car? I'm here today because my friend was going shopping, or else I'd be stuck at home."

"Oh! Here is my son, Rami." She showed me a video of her cute little boy saying "I love you, Mommy! I love you, Mommy!" as he blew kisses toward her.

"Do you see that? Isn't that beautiful? Just ten minutes ago I received a phone call from my son who was cursing at me from his father's house, calling me terrible names and just breaking my heart. I am terrified because my husband is Egyptian with dual citizenship. Here I have a good job compared to my husband. I have a good salary and make more that the hourly wage he earns. I'm pure. I have never done anything wrong. I have never been in any trouble, but this week the judge awarded my ex-husband primary custody of our son. This is so unfair. I don't understand the legal system. I don't know why I am in this situation. It is breaking my heart! What concerns me most, however, is that my ex-husband has my son's passport. Lately, whenever I see my ex-husband, he threatens me by saying that he is going to take my son to Egypt. If he takes my son to Egypt, I will never see him again.

"Do you know how badly some men in Muslim countries treat women? Have you seen the movie, *The Stoning of Soraya M.* (7)? Soraya was a wife and mother married to an Iranian man who wanted to divorce her so he could marry a fourteen year old girl. Then, instead of divorcing her as he would in America, he falsely accused her of adultery so that she would be executed, and he would not have to pay child support. The men of the town confined Soraya to a house with other women while they conducted the trial. She had no attorney and was not allowed to defend herself. Of course, they convicted her and brutally stoned her to death for a crime she did not commit."

All this time I was speechless as I listened to this woman. I realized that this interaction was not normal, to say the least. Here I was listening to the most intimate struggles of a woman married to an Egyptian man who now has primary custody of their son. This was not a random incident. This was a divine appointment.

When I work on a woman's face, often I become her confidant, as though she would speak to a doctor or a member of the clergy. Many women who come to the makeup counter have a story, even if they do not tell me what it is. Sometimes they are clearly anxious, even desperate. They want to look better. They want to feel better about themselves. I have worked on a burn victim, as well as a young girl who was trying to cover the scars on her face. I have also worked on a woman who had patches on her face with virtually no pigment left. Clients who suffer from this condition are particularly challenging because I have to remove all their makeup before doing my consultation. Exposing their skin discoloration or scarring makes them feel awkward. They want to hide. It is heartbreaking, especially if they start to cry. It can be difficult not to register any personal discomfort I may feel for them. The world can be so unkind to women when they do not conform to a cultural, subjective, and unrealistic image of perfection. This puts considerable pressure on women, particularly of Asian and Indian ancestry, where some in those cultures favor a woman with a lighter complexion.

When I work with a woman to select a foundation, my goal is to find a shade that matches her normal skin tone. In my training, I was taught to select three different foundation shades for the client - one that matches, one that is slightly darker, and one that is slightly lighter. I always know, however, that whenever I work with an Asian or Indian woman, I will have to present a foundation shade which is one to three shades lighter than her normal skin color. If I try to present a foundation that is an exact match, she will often say, "Oh, no! I am not that dark." When the shade does not match the skin color of the face, or blend with the neck, the contrast is profoundly obvious. I never understood this until one day another consultant explained to me that, in some cultures, the lighter their complexion, the higher up they are perceived to be on the social scale.

Conversely, I find it ironic that many white women have severely damaged their skin by using tanning beds, or baking at the beach with baby oil. They'd been embarrassed about their white skin. If they do not already have skin cancer, these women come to me now hoping to buy a cream to reverse the damage before it is too late. They frequently have a misconception about just how effective a jar of cream can be.

As a sales consultant, my concern is that the client will take that product home only to later return it. In this case, my only option is to accept the return as damaged goods. While my job is to make sure that it is right, it doesn't matter if it is right for me or even right at all. It matters only how the client perceives herself to look as she walks out the door.

I see this all the time. Women come in wanting to be something other than who they are. They have been conditioned to believe that how God made them is somehow not good enough.

I could see that in this woman. Her name was Rasa. She was trying to cover up exhaustion from fear and sheer panic by lightening and covering the dark discoloration under her eyes. What she needed was sleep. She needed to stop being afraid, but the circumstances were not allowing her to do that. No cosmetic was going to stop her from being afraid. No cosmetic was going to help her to sleep. For the skin to look healthy, she had to drink water, eat right, and get rest. No matter how much money she was willing to spend on cosmetics, she would never get a product that satisfies those basic needs. A cosmetic will never make her healthy or emotionally whole, nor address the traumas in her life. Yes, cosmetics can make her feel better about how she looks on the outside, but God is the only one who can truly give her an inner peace that will reflect in her eyes, her skin, and her hair.

The fact that so many women feel ashamed about the way they look is alarming to me. In extreme situations, the impact to their self-esteem can be dangerous to their well-being. I always say, "Look as good as you can." I use these cosmetics. They do work, and they serve a purpose, but they are not going to prevent your ex-husband from taking your son to Egypt. They are not going to change your skin color.

God clearly loves variety. The beauty He creates comes in all shapes, sizes, and colors. I find exceptional beauty in the different features God has given us. I enjoy encouraging women to accept and celebrate themselves as they are while making the most of their individual assets. Consider the serenity prayer: *"God, grant me the strength to accept the things I cannot change, courage to change the things that I can, and the wisdom to know the difference."* These are the basic elements for happiness in life, and none of these can be found in the bottom of a cosmetic jar.

I began to share with Rasa my personal experience with divorce and custody issues. As I was telling my story, she looked at me and said, "You are so peaceful. How are you so peaceful?"

Once again the Lord opened the door for me to say, "It's because of Christ. I am a Christian. I have given my children to the Lord. I have laid my children at the feet of Jesus. I trust God with what I can't control. I believe that He is faithful. I pray for my children. I pray for reconciliation with them. I believe that one day God is going to honor my consistent prayer, because he has given me promises. In the meantime, I try to live the noblest and most Christ-centered life I can. I try to be the best wife, best mother, and best friend I can be. I try to make my life count. I can't live someone else's life. I'm responsible and accountable for myself. To the best of my ability, I try to honor God."

She was not indicating that she was also a Christian. She most likely was Muslim. Nevertheless, I said to her, "I believe that prayer works. Through prayer, I believe God can change the hearts of people. Would you let me pray for you?"

"Would you?" Her eyes opened up at me.

"Yes," I replied, but we were not where we could do this in private as the store was relatively busy at that moment. I gave her my phone number. "Now I want you to call me. I want you to understand that God does love you and He has not abandoned you. I will be keeping you and your son Rami in my prayers."

She went on to tell me, "I love working with numbers and working in the car business; anything to do with automobiles. I graduated college with a degree in finance. Here! Here is my card."

As she handed me her card, I said, "Well, if I come across any job opportunities, I'll be sure to pass along your information."

She was very grateful. As I completed the sale, she took her products and walked away. I could tell that she was walking out with a completely different attitude than when she walked in. Her face was brighter, and her spirits lifted. She was encouraged.

It is astonishing to me that any woman would come in looking for a specific cosmetic and then share with you the agony of their life. I don't know that I'll ever see her again, but that is not the point. The point is that I know she is there, and God knows her name. When I think of her, I think of praying for the safety and protection of Rami.

I went home and watched the movie Rasa mentioned, *The Stoning of Soraya M.* I was horrified and sickened when I watched the stoning scene. The men bury Soraya up to her waist and tie her hands so that she cannot protect herself. Then they draw an arc in the ground behind which the men of the town are to stand as they throw stones. They make Soraya's father throw the first stone, but he is too old to throw with any force or accuracy. Next, Soraya's husband throws a stone, hitting her in the forehead. The force of the stone causes her upper body to fold backward while her lower body is rooted in the ground. Blood begins to flow down her face and drench her dress. Then, the husband brings his sons to the line and gives them stones to throw at their mother. The boys hesitate while the men around them shout, "Allahu Akbar!" ("God is great!") Finally, a look of determination comes into their eyes as they hurl the stones and participate in the murder of their mother. I began to understand Rasa's fear.

While modern civilized societies do not condone the stoning of women, we live in a culture where the divorce business is a huge industry. Divorcing spouses often cast stones of bitterness and hatred against each other, and will sometimes engage their children to do the same in what is known as parental alienation syndrome. The children become pawns in the character assassination of a parent. Children are gifts from God. While the parents may not be able to get along and live together, children still need and deserve a mother and a father to be present in their lives. I believe this is the will of God and why God hates divorce. Children do not deserve to carry the scars of divorce, nor should they be empowered for a lifetime as weapons in the verbal and emotional stoning of one parent. No parent should be condemned because he or she has been through a divorce. To the extent possible, the divorce process should maintain the equal role and authority of both parents in the lives of the children.

I understand as well as any woman that you cannot always choose what happens to you. You cannot make your spouse love you for the rest of your life. When a man and woman marry, they stand up to say, "For better or worse; for richer or poorer, in sickness and in health until death do us part." Obviously, not everyone is keeping these promises.

When my ex-husband and I made our vows, I believe that we fully intended to keep them. As a young couple, however, we did not know how to communicate to each other effectively, a skill we would desperately need when our trials came later. I am convinced that both God and the devil were unseen guests at our wedding. They ignored the pageantry and focused on the lofty promises we made. The devil listened and said, "Oh, really! Well, let's just see how well you do together after I turn up the heat!" Then God said, "I am here to help you because I know that there will be a five year stretch where you will bear three children, take care of sick elders, and go through a business bankruptcy. You are going to need to depend on each other and on Me. We will get through this together, if you just don't leave Me out." Unfortunately, instead of praying together, my ex-husband and I buckled under the pressure and fought constantly.

A crisis hits every marriage at some point in time, in some way. Very few people leave this life without facing a challenge bigger than they expected. You and your spouse may face a situation where it takes all the resources you have and more just to survive. Commitment is not a feeling; it is a decision. A marriage bound by commitment is a covenant, not a convenience.

Once, when speaking about wedding vows, Bishop T.D. Jakes asked in one of his messages on his program, *The Potter's Touch*, "How much poorer? What kind of sickness? Would that include mental illness?" He was exploring what it can mean to make such vows to God. For the sake of families and future generations, people entering into marriage should understand the implications of marital vows. The Bible does allow one exception as grounds for divorce - the infidelity of a spouse. Just because divorce is scripturally permissible and culturally acceptable, I don't always believe it is necessary. Couples can survive such betrayal with forgiveness and a desire to heal their marriage. In some instances, infidelity is a complete deal breaker. Bitterness, resentment and strife become strongholds until the family unit implodes. If you find yourself dealing with infidelity, I believe you have to get a word from God as to what He wants you to do. He alone knows how a partner who has failed the relationship is going to respond to the convicting power of the Holy Spirit. Some of the greatest failures have led to the greatest acts of repentance and spiritual wholeness.

A couple that is seeking restoration in their marriage will require oceans of grace and consistent prayer in order to heal. Other couples may decide to take the easy road out, thinking it is easier to get rid of somebody because they are imperfect. Do they ever consider that there is no perfect person? Author and humorist Erma Bombeck had a humorous way of expressing profound truths. She said in one of her books, "If the grass is greener on the other side, it is probably growing over a septic tank!" Everyone understands that fertilizer makes grass greener.

I pray for this woman and her son. Her life is in turmoil, and is unlikely to improve soon unless she and her husband can somehow reconcile. Although she is young and educated, long-term stress this intense could negatively impact her health, appearance, and self-esteem. The effects are already apparent under her eyes. She still faces the possibility of divorce, raising a child alone, or worse, the kidnapping of her son, not to mention the biases she faces as a Iranian woman either in her own culture or in the American culture. The help I could give her at the makeup counter is marginal and temporary. The best advice I could give her is to pray often, and comfort herself in the knowledge that God loves her now and forever. She would face no condemnation in Christ. Embracing this truth, she is better able to love herself in the skin that God gave her.

Dear Daddy, I understand that life is not fair. Please forgive me for any harm I may have caused. My mistakes are so far beneath what You intend for my life. You made no mistakes when You created me. Conform me to Your image. This is accomplished when my mind is renewed by Your Holy Spirit and Your Word. Heal my wounds that have been inflicted by the judgmental acts of others. Help me to walk in forgiveness toward them and myself.

Where my children are involved, teach me to lay down my defenses. Help me to understand that they did not ask to be here. Help me to lay aside my need to be right or to justify myself. I will stand one day before You and give an account of the life that I have lived before them. The power of my influence is great. Shield their hearts. Comfort them. Comfort me. I realize that the world does not revolve around me, but that my world should revolve around You.

Where there has been a breech in my family relationships, by Your power, show me ways to build a bridge. Soften hearts. Reveal to me my own human frailties and my need for You. Help me to understand that this bridge will be built across the body of the Lord Jesus Christ, who spanned the gulf between God and man. He purchased my peace. He purchased my redemption. Help me to realize that because of His sacrifice, I am able to walk across that great divide, back into fellowship with You and my family. If I am open, this process can begin today. I am praying and believing that it will.

In Jesus' name, so be it! Amen.

Makeup Lesson 13: Your Makeup Personality

The remaining makeup lessons shift from skin care to makeup artistry. The following questions will help you determine your makeup personality: mostly A's = Minimalist; mostly B's = Confident; mostly C's = Daring.

Some people choose to wear makeup to enhance their best feature. Others may use it to help camouflage minor skin discolorations or blemishes. Still others have fun playing with color and enjoy experimenting with makeup's ability to transform. Each of us has a desired look that we want to achieve, and definitions of that look can vary.

1. How much time do you spend applying makeup in the morning?
   A. 0-5 minutes
   B. 5-15 minutes
   C. More than 15 minutes

2. How many products do you use to achieve your look?
   A. 0-4
   B. 4-10
   C. More than 10

3. What is the overall effect you hope to achieve by wearing makeup?
   A. Cover minor imperfections, but look natural.
   B. Enhance some of my favorite features and look polished and put together.
   C. Create a little drama, playing up the eyes, lips, cheeks, or all three.

Most people will have a dominant makeup personality. Many, however, will be comfortable expressing different personalities in different situations. For example, the same person could be a Minimalist when she goes to work out at the gym, a Confident when she goes to the office during the week, or a Daring when she attends a holiday party. Understanding the concept of makeup personality may give you the confidence to explore new looks with makeup in ways you would never have considered before.

My Makeup Personality is ________________________________

Lesson #14

Going Home

Debbie is an extraordinarily beautiful woman. She started working in the fragrance department in January about six months after I started in cosmetics. We hit it off instantly, which was fortunate because I had been offered an opportunity to fly back to my childhood home in New Jersey to sing at a special event. It would be a long weekend trip, and I needed someone to cover my schedule. One of my coworkers gave me Debbie's phone number suggesting that she needed the hours; she had recently separated from her husband.

I called Debbie and explained my situation. Her immediate response was, "You're a singer? Oh, I love to sing. I grew up singing in the church."

"Did you really?"

"Yes. I started as a child. Through my teenage years and early twenties, I sang in the choir every Sunday. I even sang in competitions," Debbie reminisced.

"I also grew up singing in church," I said. "My father was a preacher and a pianist. When I was very young, my parents realized I could harmonize with them. We became a singing trio. I remember when I was five years old my father would put me on a chair to sing my solo so the audience could see me."

"That's wonderful, Peggy! The singing ministry is a tradition in my family, too. In fact, my great, great grandfather wrote some of the hymns you probably sang as a child."

"Really! Which ones?"

"Let me see...Do you know *Just as I Am?*"

"Of course!"

"I'm sure you know *Jesus Loves Me This I Know.*"

"Absolutely! That's amazing. These are some of the most famous hymns ever written. It sure is a small world."

"Yes. Boy, that takes me back. Well, I'll be glad to cover for you at work. What are your hours next weekend?"

Thanks to Debbie I got my shift covered.

And thanks to my mother-in-law, I got my flight covered. I had told her about receiving a message from one of my old high school friends. She told me that my high school was organizing an event in January to raise money for music scholarships. For the event, the school was inviting alumni to come back to perform with current students at an evening concert. While there were no so-called magnet schools in the 1970's, my high school happened to draw a lot of students who were oriented toward the performing arts, music, singing, and theater. Today, funding for art's education is a challenge in many public school districts across the country. My high school was trying to fill the funding gap. This was a creative way to do it.

Many talented students had followed me since my graduation forty years ago. As my friend told me, however, the organizers of the event identified two alumni whom they specifically wanted to appear at the event – Jim Hynes, a good friend of mine who is a world-renowned trumpet player, and myself. Even though I was very flattered, I wasn't sure I would be able to make it. Jim lived north of New York City. I knew it would be easy for him to go if his schedule allowed it. It would be good to see him again. I was hesitating because of the cost. Where would I stay? Would I need to rent a car? My mother-in-law was insistent. She said, "Peggy, you have to go. This is just an incredible opportunity. You'll never have another chance to do this."

When she offered to pay for the airfare, I contacted other friends from my high school days. My precious friend, Kären, and I used to perform musicals together. She was now married to a dentist. "Sure, you can stay here. My daughter is living in L.A, pursuing an acting career. You can stay in her room."

Another friend of mine from high school owned a limousine service with her husband. "Peggy, you're coming back! I can't wait to see you! Do you want me to pick you up at the airport? When do you arrive?"

So God made a way for me. As I was sitting in the plane flying to New Jersey, my mind was flooding with memories. It was amazing to consider that I would be performing again on that high school stage. I thought about the last time I performed at my high school while my father was alive. I was sixteen, and it was late spring. School would be out soon. We were performing our final show for the year. The auditorium was packed. I had a few singing parts that night, but I remember vividly my solo finale. I sang *Oh, Happy Day!* with a choir backup. I remember standing on that platform, looking out and seeing my father sitting in the front row. He was so ill that night. His ability to stand and move on his own was almost gone. There were already nine times in my life that my mother and I thought he was about to die, but he always rallied.

Oh, Happy Day! is a great song for audience participation. Everyone was singing and clapping that day. The house was rocking. When it was over, I got a standing ovation. As I looked at my father, I saw him put his hand on my mother. My mother then turned around to lift my father out of his seat. For the rest of my life, I will remember being in that auditorium, and seeing him look at me with profound love in his eyes while he gave me a standing ovation.

Just a year before that night, when I was fifteen, my father was well enough to take me to Israel,

Holland, and Greece. I remembered him saying to me during that trip, "Sweetheart, I asked the Lord to let me live to see my fortieth year in ministry. It was always my heart's desire to go to the Holy Land before I die. I am so grateful to God to be able to share this experience with you."

I had no way of knowing that, after this performance, my father would finally go to be with the Lord in July. Forty years later, I was home again on my high school stage performing *Hero* (Mariah Carey, 1993), backed up by the same man who was the head of the music department when I was a student there. I was singing for my father, who was a brilliant musician, a spiritual giant, and my hero.

Everyone agreed the concert was a success. Afterwards, about fifteen of my old friends and I went out to celebrate at a local restaurant. The next day, Kären, took me into the city to a fantastic restaurant for dinner followed by a Broadway musical. The entire weekend was magical.

I had a suitcase full of feelings that weekend. People say you can never go home again. I think you can. In my case, however, I was coming home forty years later a radically different person. As I met old friends, I thought about how thankful I was for all the teachers who helped me graduate a year early so that I could go to New York to take voice lessons. I was thankful for my mother who worked so hard after my father died, and moved with me to New York City so that I could go to the American Academy to get my education.

Here I was working retail and doing makeovers on women. Then, with two week's notice I was standing in New Jersey reflecting on all the people who had helped me to become who I am. I recognized at that moment that God knew me. He knew all the elements of my make up. He knew that I loved singing. He knew that I loved performing and producing. He was not asking me to sacrifice that part of me. He was taking me back to affirm my gifts and show me that He loves me and has never forgotten me.

This was another confirmation that you cannot out-give God. When you give of yourself to others, when you give encouragement and love, God will make a way to give back to you. When He gives back to you, He can pile a bigger portion on you than you ever imagined. The best thing you can do for people is to sow encouragement into their lives and believe in them. I had been spending months in the makeup department encouraging women, telling them how beautiful they were and making them feel special. I was telling them that God could get them through all kinds of situations and that He had great plans for them. I was doing makeovers as a tool to share the grace of God with people. Here I was now, the recipient of God's grace in a way that I never thought would happen.

God is intimately aware of us - every part of us. He can take us back in time. We get to have makeup lessons. We can have a chance to say thank you to people who helped us along the way. We can have another chance to love people whom we thought were lost to us. God's grace will allow us the opportunity to do some things over.

As they called me to the stage that night, I knew that my parents were watching me. I felt them standing up for me once again. I knew I was a reflection of all the gifts and talents I inherited from them - the love for God, the love for service, and the love for people. I have used these gifts and talents in a multitude of ways over the years.

I like to think that we are all like prisms. God holds us up and turns us. He shines His light through us. Every time He turns us a different way, the light is split into the different colors of His love, grace, and mercy for people. Every day we have the choice to be God's reflection on the earth.

Dear Daddy, people say you can never go home again. I am grateful that You have given me a picture of reconciliation and restoration in the Scriptures, where the prodigal son was able to go home to his father. The prodigal son wasted his resources and came home asking to be a servant, but was welcomed as a son. As the Father of the prodigal child, Your arms are open wide, and You are ever looking for me and waiting for me to be reconciled to You.

There may be times when I "go home" to some people, and I will not be well received. In those moments, pour in Your grace and healing power. Give me the ability to rise above the hurt and disappointment, while I continue to believe and pray for reconciliation. I am thankful that I can always run home into Your arms.

Daddy, please help me to be the kind of Christian who stands with arms open wide. Help certain people in my life to know that when they have true repentance, they can come home to me, and expect acceptance and restoration. Daddy, You have forgiven me of so much in my life. Remind me of that fact when I deal with others. You said in Your Word that You desire mercy over judgment. Help me to be merciful and longsuffering the same way that You have responded to me.

Shield my heart and my emotions. Prepare the hearts of others to receive the love I have to give. One day, I will go home to be with You. Until that day, teach me how to be a safe place for others. No broken relationship is beyond Your power to heal.

Thank You in advance for the victory. In Jesus' name, so be it! Amen.

Makeup Lesson 14: Concealer

($) Every woman has flaws. Frequently a client will come in with a specific area of concern that she wants to cover up. For example, I often see young women with acne coming in with layers of makeup on their faces. I have known women who expect a foundation to cover their wrinkles or to cover very deep discolorations on their face due to scarring or to black circles under the eyes.

There are two steps to deal with these issues. First, treat the underlying problem area. Second, conceal the effects. One is not a substitute for the other.

A **Treatment** is meant to correct a problem. It is specific. It is not makeup. You must not confuse the expectations of each product, and you cannot exchange one for the other.

A **Concealer** will cover over a problem. It is best applied with a **Concealer Brush**, with a stroke known as stippling, which is a press and pulling motion. Lightly press the product onto the skin and gently pull to blend. Always target a specific area. The color should be close to the color of the natural skin. If it is too light, it can appear grey. If it is too dark, it appears as another discoloration.

The foundation is then applied over the concealer in such a way at that it doesn't drag off the product you carefully placed over the area of concern.

There are eye creams which will lighten and brighten the skin under the eye, for example. These may minimize the concern, but not totally eliminate it. The cause may be genetic or hereditary, thus the need for a concealer. Acne needs to be treated with a regimen that may require medical assistance. The ClarisonicTM is a deep cleansing machine which helps to clean out pores along with assisting with other concerns. Rosacea is a skin condition that causes the skin to look as though it is sunburned. There are color-correcting creams that can neutralize the appearance of Rosacea. Some concealers claim to contain treatment, however, I would not use these products as a substitute for treatment.

Lesson #15

Take Authority

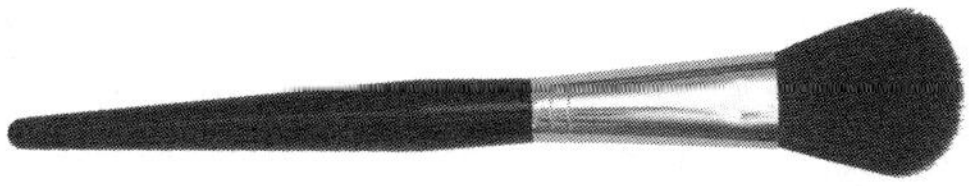

I recall that soon after I returned from New Jersey, management transferred Debbie from the fragrance department to the cosmetics department. We frequently had the same evening shift, so we had a lot of time to stand around and talk during the slow hours late at night. I soon realized that Debbie had only recently left her husband of ten years. They had a son together. She had primary custody.

"Peggy, God has been dealing with me for a long time about wandering so far from Him. I feel that He has been trying to bring me back to church, but it's been hard because my husband is an atheist. I mean my 'ex-husband.'"

"Was he an atheist when you married him?"

"Yes, but in the beginning, we never talked about religion. I hadn't been to church much since my first divorce. I guess I was just glad to have someone love me again. I still love my husband. Really, I do, but over the years he has become so very hostile toward me about God, and angry at the church."

"So, you're saying that he's not just an intellectual atheist," I asked.

"No, he's not. I mean, Peggy, it's been just horrible. He does things which make me uncomfortable. He doesn't even try to hide it from me. It has been so bad that I felt I was going to lose my soul if I stayed with him any longer."

"I'm so sorry to hear that."

"I'm in an apartment now with my son. Even though my ex-husband is wealthy, he doesn't give me much child support. I needed a job, so here I am, trying to find myself again. I'm trying to find my way back."

"It's interesting, Debbie, that you come from a ministry background. I believe there is ministerial legacy that's passed down to each generation. There's no way that you can fall so far from the grace of God that His arm isn't long enough to pull you back from the pit. What church did you attend growing up?"

"My family went to a Southern Baptist church. I grew up on a ranch in Oklahoma. When I go to see them, we still get together to sing around the piano. In fact, I have a video of my family. My mother is playing the piano, and we're all singing. Those are the sweetest memories I have growing up. I had the greatest parents. Would you like to see it?"

Debbie took out her smartphone and scrolled through the images to find the video. In it, she was with her mother, aunt and uncle, and some other family members all singing together. It reminded me so much of my own precious memories. Like Debbie, I sometimes wondered how in the world I ever ended up here.

In Louisiana, they eat frogs' legs. I have been told that the way to cook them is to put the frogs into a pot of lukewarm water, then gradually turn up the heat. This puts the frogs to sleep. When the water boils, the frogs are dead, and the legs are cooked.

From my own experience, I have observed that deception works the same way - gradually. First, you are introduced to the lie. It may be either the lie someone tells you or the lie you tell yourself. If it were a blatant lie, you would jump right out of the situation, much like the frog that is put into a pot of boiling water. Deception is a setup by the enemy. Scripture says, "*There is a way which seems right to a man and appears straight before him, but at the end of it is the way of death*" (Proverbs 16:25). The same Satan who seduces you in the first place is the one who laughs at you from the corner of the room while you are sitting in divorce court, ill with a disease, or addicted to a substance that has a death grip on you. You name the price. In truth, the temporary benefits achieved by deception are never worth what you pay for them in the end.

"Oh, Peggy, I have gotten so far off track," Debbie whimpered.

"That's okay. You're moving in the right direction now. God's calling you back because He has His hand on your life."

"I have been to a couple of different churches around here, but I haven't found one for me yet. What church do you go to, Peggy?"

"My husband and I go to a non-denominational church. They have a wonderful music ministry. We would love to meet you at a service sometime."

"Okay. Maybe on a weekend when my son goes to see his father."

"You know, we have a youth service at the same time. Your son would be welcome to a service with people his own age."

"That could be a good idea. You know, I'm so concerned about my son. I tried so hard with my daughter, but it hasn't worked out as I'd hoped."

"You have a daughter, too?" I asked.

"Yes. She got into serious trouble with drugs a couple of years ago. Thank God, it looks like she has beaten her addiction. Then she got pregnant last year. Not married. Now I'm a grandmother. Fortunately, the baby is in good health. My daughter and the baby are living with the father's parents. Thank God his mother is a devout Christian who prays for them and loves them unconditionally. She has been good to my daughter. My ability to assist them financially is limited, of course. I'm struggling to get back on my own feet financially. I came to work here because I had to have a job somewhere in order to eat and pay the bills. I'm grateful, however, in my little apartment. I don't have nearly the creature comforts I used to have, but I have peace. I finally have peace in my life.

"But, I still love that man. I don't know why I love him, but I do. Sometimes though, when he talks to me the words that come out of his mouth are so crippling. I couldn't take it anymore."

"Debbie, there is the power of life and death in the tongue (Proverbs 18:21). If your ex-husband is constantly putting you down, it is understandable why you did what you did, not just for your sake, but for your son's sake. You still love him, but you want him to be something he isn't, a godly husband, and you want your son to grow up to be a godly husband to his wife someday. We have to pray for him. I know you're so badly hurt that it's hard for you to do that right now. I'll pray that God will heal your heart and give you the ability to forgive him. This is a process. It won't happen overnight. Your feelings are understandable. You're wounded. He will always have a place of influence in your son's life, so we have to pray a hedge of protection around your son. God can save your ex. Nothing is too hard for God. In the meantime, I will pray for God to shield your heart whenever you have to deal with him."

We went home that night after our shift. The next week we were both working again. Even though there were customers in the store, it was quiet by my bay. As I was standing at my counter, I happened to notice Debbie move toward the phone in her bay to take a call. I don't know what happened or what the caller said, but she was completely silent. When she hung up the phone, she turned and looked at me. Her face was ashen and she started to sob. As I looked at her, I could see that she was shattering emotionally, as a glass window shatters into a thousand shards. I have had this happen to me where someone has spoken to me with such venom, such soul-piercing condemnation. It's demonic. The same thing was happening to this beautiful woman, right in the middle of the floor. There was no privacy, nowhere to go. She was deeply embarrassed.

I called over to her, "Debbie!" Debbie walked over to me. She stood there and looked at me. She couldn't talk. There was such panic in her face, such dejection in her eyes. She was wilting like a parched flower. It was so horrible to see. I knew how she was feeling. It didn't matter that we were in the middle of a department store. I didn't even think about it, but I instinctively reached out and scooped her into my arms to hold her. She was sobbing.

I said, *"Jesus, Jesus! Debbie, you listen to me. I don't know what happened, but in the name of Jesus I bind that spirit of rejection and hurt in the name of Jesus and I command you, Satan, to release your attack on her right now. I plead the blood of Jesus over your heart, mind, body, soul, and spirit. Satan, you get your hands off her, in the name of Jesus. I draw a circle of the bloodline of Jesus around her heart, and I forbid the enemy to cross over that bloodline."*

I found myself feeling very militant. I felt as though there was something there that I wanted to strike at, but it was nothing I could see. Nevertheless, I was taking authority over its attack on Debbie through my prayer.

It was the strangest thing. In an instant after that quick prayer for Debbie, she pulled away and looked at me. She quickly dried her tears. She looked as stunned as I felt. She stared at me and said, "Thank you, Peggy. Thank you!"

I have had a similar experience where someone had spoken such evil words over me, and someone else was there to yank me back from the pit. I don't know how to explain it, but we were both deeply aware in that moment of the spiritual battle going on around us. She understood that she was reacting to something that was not of this world and that there is such power in prayer. The contrast of the negative words spoken to her and the positive words of God over her at that moment was completely apparent.

The Word of God says, *"The earnest, heartfelt prayer of a righteous man or woman makes tremendous power available"* (James 5:16). What is earnest, heartfelt, praying? When you engage in spiritual warfare, and you see someone taking an emotional nosedive, there is nothing you can say or do to fix the situation. You cannot take demonically inspired words back. Instead, you curse those words to nullify their effect. You have the guts to say, "Excuse me, Satan! That's not going to happen on my watch," and pull those words out by the root, so they don't grow into the heart of the person hearing them. You take spiritual dominion over the circumstance. You go to war against an invisible ancient adversary, and take no prisoners. Simply praying the Word of God back to Him is a tremendously powerful weapon against the enemy, but you have to pray earnestly and with heart.

My whole life I have been such a "fixer". I have tried so hard to fix a long list of situations, particularly for my children. I don't know, though, that I have ever fixed anything. For the last year, I have stopped trying to fix everything. Now I am more effective by praying for people. This realization should not surprise me when I understand that God has already specified, *"If My people … shall humble themselves, pray, seek, crave … My face and turn from their wicked ways, then will I … forgive their sin, and heal their land"* (2 Chronicles 7:14). Nowhere in this statement does God ask us to fix anything or anyone. He does the forgiving, the healing, and the fixing when we remain humble, repentant, and prayerful.

I don't know who was more startled, Debbie or me. It happened so quickly. I did this because I have been her. I know how it feels to get a phone call in a public place and be reamed by the words of an unexpected caller. You can't go home because you need the money. You can't lose your job because you have to eat. And you can't go hide anywhere else. It would have taken Debbie a good five to seven minutes to get to a private place. Even the bathroom was on the upper floor. So where was Debbie going to go? What was she going to do? Sometimes you cannot pray for yourself. Sometimes you are that low. The beautiful thing is that God knew what was going to happen. I was scheduled to be there with her exactly at that moment when she needed me. God knew what she was going to face before she faced it.

"Thank you, Peggy," Debbie said again. "It wouldn't look very good if I were trying to sell make-up and mascara were running down my cheek, now would it?"

"No, I guess not. You're welcome, sweetheart."

Debbie went back to work completely composed, finished her shift and went home. A couple of days later we were working together again. She brought me a card and I opened it. The front of the card showed a picture of a movie actress all decked out for a premiere. The sentiment inside read, "If praise and encouragement were accessories, you'd be rockin' the red carpet." My eyes welled up, and I hugged her tightly.

"I can't tell you what your prayer meant to me the other day."

"Debbie, God loves you. You may have walked away from Him, but He has never walked away from you. He knew what was going to happen to you that day, and He had provision for you."

"The phone call was from my ex-husband. He likes to play with my emotions by telling me how he wants to get back together, but then he'll call me like he did the other day and just crush me."

"Debbie, you walked away from your husband. You walked away because there wasn't any unity in the relationship. Scripture teaches us that light and darkness have no fellowship together (2 Corinthians 6:14). They cannot co-exist. They cancel each other out. If God wanted you back in that relationship, there would be a definite sign. The sign wouldn't be in you. It would be in his changing relationship with the Lord. Sometimes we try to open doors that God has already closed. That is what I say when God pries my fingers off things. I may be unwilling to let go, but God is the loving parent who says to me, 'I will get you to let this go, either the easy way or the hard way. It is up to you how you want to do this.' Don't make God pry your fingers off this relationship, Debbie. It's more painful that way. Let go. Solomon writes that to everything there is a season; a time to break down and a time to build up; a time to embrace and a time to refrain from embracing. (Ecclesiastes 3:1-8). Sometimes separation leads to restoration. Some people never appreciate what they have until they've lost it."

I keep Debbie's card on my dresser. Her card is one of the greatest compliments I have ever received in my life. That card tells me that no matter how beautiful people may see me on the outside, Debbie appreciates the quality of my spirit and compares it to the expensive jewels an actress might wear on the red carpet. The fruit of the Holy Spirit was so profound to Debbie that day. In her mind, it is worth millions. When Debbie said that I had given her something priceless, that "something" was God within me showing up for her. The only thing that is special about any of us is the Christ within us that people see. When someone is hurting that badly, you can transfer the power of the Holy Spirit through Christ living in you. I remember how devastated I felt as a single mother thirteen years ago when my spirit was crushed at work. Just as my pastors arrived on time to encourage me then, now I am the one who is there to tell Debbie, "You are going to get through this. You will get past this. You will, because God never gives up on His investments."

Several months later, as we were about to close, Debbie asked two other consultants and me to make a circle around her to pray over her. I was happy to hear Debbie report that her husband was pursuing her and asking her to come home. She had been noticing a significant change in his behavior. It seems that Debbie's husband had a friend at work who had been talking with him about the goodness of the Lord. He was softening toward her, as well as becoming more considerate and respectful. We were supportive and cautiously optimistic. Debbie said she believed she needed to be home full-time for the sake of her son. She made her boundaries clear to her husband: Don't disrespect my God, my family or me anymore. She felt God calling her to go home and stand for her marriage.

Debbie quit soon after that night. Several weeks later I met her for lunch. She had a beautiful new diamond ring on her hand, and was encouraged in her heart that the Lord was working to heal her family.

Dear Daddy, You said in Your Word that I could come boldly to Your throne to find grace and help in time of trouble. Therefore, I come before You as your child who has been redeemed by the blood of my elder brother, Jesus. On the authority of Your Word and my birthright, I submit my life to You.

Satan, I resist you in the name of Jesus and on the authority of the Word of God. I command you to take your hands off everything that pertains to me. Release my body, mind, soul, and spirit. You were defeated at Calvary over two thousand years ago.

Daddy, I claim my life for You in the name of Jesus. I speak peace and restoration over myself in every way. You are Jehovah Nissi, my warrior God, who fights on my behalf. You are Jehovah Shalom, my peace which passes understanding.

I ask You to save me now. I want to be born again. I ask You to heal every part of my life. Deliver me from evil. Carry me through my dark hours and give me the wisdom and understanding in the trials I face.

I believe that You hear me, and I seal this prayer with Your signet ring, dipped in the blood of Jesus and given to me.

I decree this and say it so. Amen.

Makeup Lesson 15: Foundation

($$) There are numerous types of foundations in every line. When choosing a foundation, consider the amount of coverage you desire and the color to match your skin. You may also want to consider the addition of sunscreen to the foundation product.

Foundations can be in a cream, powder, mousse, or liquid form. You can apply a foundation with a brush, an air brush, a puff, or a sponge. You can use a foundation by itself or in conjunction with another form. For instance, you may start with a base coat of cream, liquid, or mousse and then finish with a brush on powder foundation. If you apply that in the morning, you only have to bring the powder foundation with you for touch-ups later in the day.

The use of a primer preceding your foundation is a wonderful tool, which provides a beautiful canvass for the foundation. It is typically oil free and smoothes out any imperfections on the skin. The foundation will look as though it is velvety in texture.

The choice of foundation is based on the sheer or fullness of the coverage you desire. You may change the foundation with the seasons. For instance, if you live in a very hot climate, you may want a more sheer coverage in the summer. You will also choose the finish you want to achieve, such as a matte, or dewy look. Clients with very oily skin may like a powder foundation. Clients who are prone to very dry skin will appreciate a more radiant finish.

The color should match your skin tone as closely as possible. You do not want a dark mark which distinguishes between your face and your neck. You do not want your face to be lighter than your neck. The objective is to create a seamless line between your neck and face. If your neck is significantly darker than your face, the objective will be to create consistency between the two areas.

There are also tinted moisturizers and BB creams to wear for a light finish or when engaging in athletic activities. Sunscreen in foundation is beneficial, even critical if you are not using a sunscreen separately. Foundation is most attractive when applied with the correct tool. Your fingers will work, but it is not the best approach. Invest in a good set of brushes.

Lesson #16

Maximize Your Assets

After my lunch break, I noticed two women in their fifties over by the lipstick testers. They were trying on different samples. I walked over and greeted them.

"Oh! Hello. We were just trying on some lipstick," one of them said as she fumbled slightly while she put the lipstick sample back into its slot. "Do you think you could help me pick a color that would be right for me?"

"Sure," I said. "Let's see…let's try this one. That one could be interesting also. If you would like to take a seat, I'll get my brush and put some on for you."

"Would you?" She was slightly unsure in her reply.

"It would be my pleasure!" I got my brush kit and started to apply the lipstick. I would back away so that she could take a look at herself in the mirror.

"Oh, my! That's so pretty!"

"Yes, it's very nice. What's your name, ma'am?"

"Elisa."

"Elisa, why don't we also try some blush today? Are you up for that?"

"I would like that very much. I'm out for the afternoon with my sister. I haven't been out of the house much in several months. I'm afraid I haven't taken very good care of myself."

"Elisa, you don't have to apologize to me for the way you look. Why don't we start from the beginning? If you'll let me, I'll just take your makeup off and use a nice cleanser. Then we'll just play for a little bit. Sometimes, that makes you feel better. It's a good pick-me-up."

I started working on her face and added the blush. "You know, Elisa, you have beautiful brown eyes," I said. "Honestly, makeup is mostly about maximizing your assets and minimizing your flaws. As I look at you, I would say that your eyes are your most attractive feature. Do you ever use eye makeup or mascara or anything like that?"

"No, not really."

"Would you like to try some?"

This time, she didn't hesitate. "Okay!"

After each application of makeup, she would look at herself in the mirror and say with surprise, "Ooooh!" Her sister would also take a look and gush, "Elisa! You look so beautiful!!" I was smiling while they were giggling with excitement.

"Elisa, most people don't pay attention to their eyes. They'll use a little rouge or blush or lip color, but they don't do much with their eyes. They don't realize that the eyes and the eyebrows are the most expressive part of the face. Everyone has heard that the eyes are the window to the soul. If you want to hide someone's identity in a picture, what do you do? You cover the eyes with a black strip. People are drawn to what they see in your eyes, and your eyebrows are like the frame of a painting. Women shouldn't be afraid to use eye makeup. If you like a dramatic look, you can use bold, vivid colors and large strokes. If you like a minimal look, then you can use soft, neutral colors. Either way creates a nice effect so that your eyes will stand out, and people will focus on them when they look at you. You have beautiful eyes, Elisa. You should do this."

When I finished applying the eye shadow, she looked at me and beamed, "I just feel like a million bucks!"

"Well, you *look* like a million bucks."

"This is terrific! I can't tell you what a blessing this has been to me today. You really have been a blessing."

When she started to use those words, the way she repeated the word "blessing", I understood that she and her sister were more than likely Christians. "I'm glad to have been a blessing to you today. Are you and your sister Christians?"

"Yes, we certainly are. You have meant so much to me today. I haven't been out of the house in months. I have been struggling because I haven't been able to eat. I've had stomach issues, and I haven't been able to keep food down. I have been terribly discouraged. My sister came over today to rescue me out of my house. She insisted we get out and get a change of scenery. So here we are at the mall and we're here to have some fun. When I walked in here, I just felt so low. Now I'm walking out of here, and I feel beautiful!"

"And you look beautiful, too. Would you…May I ask you if it would be okay for me to pray for you?"

She looked at me so stunned. "Would you do that?"

"Absolutely! We can stand here right now while I put on the finishing touches. I can pray for you and people won't know the difference." Elisa took a deep breath to focus.

> *"God, I am asking You to heal Elisa's stomach. I am asking You to touch her and bless her from the top of her head to the tip of her toes. I don't know what is causing this, but You are the Great Physician. This is not too hard for You. I rebuke every demonic assignment against her in the name of Jesus, and I call for ministering, warring angels to come to her assistance right now as I speak. Minister to her physically, emotionally, psychologically, spiritually, and financially. Draw her close to You in a special way.*
>
> *I pray this in Jesus' name. So be it."*

The Word says that we are supposed to lay hands on the sick, and they will recover. By touching her face and applying makeup while I was praying for her, technically speaking, I was laying my hands on her. Working the makeup counter, I can lay hands on people all the time and pray without them ever knowing it. Laying hands on someone and praying for them does not necessarily require a priest or pastor and a church building. I am often humbled in my line of work. When I am gently applying makeup, I am frequently touching someone's face. I am touching their eyes. I'm touching their mouth. My touch and my words often produce a palpable response, as though I am transferring energy to them. I believe I am transferring spiritual power to them, even if the person does not realize that I am praying for them while I am applying makeup. Sometimes I have a sense that a certain person has their guard up and would not be comfortable with me approaching them openly about the Lord. I have gotten to the place, however, where I can still pray for them as I touch their face or eyes. While I am doing my job quietly applying makeup, I still pray to God, *Please bless this person. Please take care of this person. You know their needs and concerns.*

In Elisa's case, she didn't mind that I was praying for her. I finished praying as I finished her makeup. Elisa's sister was cute. She got so excited that she interjected, "Okay, please let me take a picture. I have to take a picture of you, Elisa."

Elisa was looking in the mirror saying, "I don't think I can wash my face. What am I going to do? I can't wash my face when I go home."

Smiling, I said, "Of course, you can, Elisa. You don't have to buy all these products now. Start with this, and just get the basics. Then, gradually add more."

All the while, Elisa's sister was snapping photos. "Elisa, I've got to get a picture of you and Peggy."

As I was posing with Elisa, she said to her sister, "You need to sit down. Peggy needs to give you a makeover, too!" So the sister sat down. As I was giving her a makeover, Elisa was watching. When I finished with the sister, Elisa was taking pictures of her. Of course, I had to pose with the sister.

When we finished, Elisa walked out of there saying, "I feel like I'm walking on air. I feel like I'm floating."

I knew it was not me. I knew it was God. He uses us to touch other people, but we limit Him when we are too afraid to reach out. We may think they are going to be offended or uncomfortable. The biggest surprise to me is that when I ask people if I can pray for them, the majority are, of course, surprised, then flattered, humbled, and amazed that a stranger would care about them. It takes them a moment to process what is going on, but the reaction has never been negative in my experience. It has always been positive.

Youth in our society is celebrated. The image of perfection is celebrated. When women reach a certain age, they may begin to think, *Oh, why bother? It's no good. It's all downhill from here.* I believe it is specifically important for women who are in their 40's, 50's, and older to realize that it is good to take care of themselves at every age. When you take a woman like Elisa and begin to do a transformation, she starts to understand how wonderful it feels to look good and be the best she can be. No, she is never going to be twenty again, however, a woman can be beautiful at every age. You always do it by maximizing your best features and minimizing the visual appearance of flaws and imperfections. This is exactly what God does. God always wants to show you off. He is always maximizing your strengths. He is also so quick to cover your imperfections with His mercy and grace. That's how God does makeovers on you. He does the same thing from the inside out.

Dear Daddy, You said I would prosper and be in good health, even as my soul prospers. My eyes are the reflection of the condition of my soul. When people look into my eyes, help them to see a reflection of You. Help me to understand that there is no such thing as a "chance" meeting. With You, there are no accidents, only incidents.

I ask You to bring my body, soul, and spirit under the authority of the Holy Spirit. I speak to every system in my body and command it to answer to You, in the name of Jesus. You are the Great Physician. You are the Great Healer. You are capable of ministering to every physical, emotional, and psychological concern that I have.

Thank You that Jesus died to redeem me from my sin, and to bring me healing and deliverance in this present world. You are the final authority in my life. My times are in Your hands. I will live to declare the glory of the Lord to future generations. I will live to complete the assignment You have for me in the earth.

Give me wisdom as to how I should eat. Make clear the behavioral changes that I should make to contribute to my well-being. Give me the strength to discipline my body and bring it under the control of the Holy Spirit. Motivate me to exercise appropriately and to rest my body when I need it. If I need medical treatment, please lead me to the right physicians and hospitals. Give me the ability to discern Your voice in their recommendations. Ultimately, I am in charge of the body You gave me. Help me to know the correct strategy to take.

Protect me by Your power. Give me the desire to pray for others, that my prayer of faith will raise them up. If the healing and restoration process takes time, please help me to be patient and consistent in my prayer and praise. Some battles are not won overnight. I speak to the enemy Satan on the authority of the Word of God and command him to release his attack on my body, soul, and spirit. He has no legal right to my territory.

I thank You, Daddy, that You hear me, and I boldly confess that I will walk in all that Jesus died to give me. I will join my faith with others that they will be able to do the same.

I decree and declare these things, in Jesus' name. So be it! Amen.

Makeup Lesson 16: Blush

($) The purpose of blush is to bring the skin to life. It should not be overpowering; it should enhance your appearance.

The best blush cosmetics come with three colors. First, take a good quality makeup brush to apply the primary color using a backward "C", starting on the cheek underneath the middle of the eye to the right or left of the nose and stroke backwards on an angle toward the ear. The second color will be a darker bronze or a darker pigment of the color blush. Apply this underneath the primary color to accentuate the cheek bone and to give definition. You may also use this color on the jaw line and the chin with a downward motion. The third color is a very light bronze, almost a cream color. This shade acts as a highlighter and goes above the primary color in a sweeping downward motion under the eyes to brighten the eye area.

If you are a Minimalist, you do not have to use all three steps. Feel free to choose the primary color only, applied lightly. You may also apply a light cream blush as opposed to powder. Just remember that cream blush should follow cream foundation and powder blush over powder. However, if you are anticipating a special evening out, I recommend you consider trying the three color blush approach to give yourself that complete and defined look.

Many women struggle with the application of blush and bronzer. They have trouble locating the cheek bone. Follow these steps: 1. Smile. 2. Locate the center of the apple of the cheek and place your index finger there. 3. Place your thumb at the top of the ear where it connects to your head. 4. Take your thumb and bring it toward your index finger. The bone you feel will be the cheekbone.

Use separate brushes for your bronzer and blush. You won't confuse the colors with any remnant of each. This will make each color more distinct. If your veins tend toward blue, choose a cool color blush. If your veins tend toward green, choose a neutral or warm color blush. Choose lip colors and eye shadow colors that are in the same family. You want to create a complete look where each part of the face is enhanced and not competing with the other for attention.

Lesson #17

Love That Sticks

I believe that all my extraordinary experiences with clients have been divinely ordered. I know they were extraordinary because my coworkers have told me that their experiences with customers are rarely like mine. Certainly, not every woman who came up to my counter presented an opportunity for me to pray for them. My spirit leapt inside me only when I saw something unusual or odd, such as the woman with growths on her face, or the Asian student who couldn't fail. It felt as though God was saying to me, "Okay, it's time for another lesson." Sometimes the lesson was for them. God had put me in a place where He could use me to share His love for other people. Sometimes, however, the lesson was for me.

Frequently when women come into our department, they are upset about the way they look. They want the best wrinkle cream, or the most expensive new product on the market that can stop the aging process. They are worried about their sagging skin or their wrinkled eyes. We see a lot of insecure women. Also, a department store is not the same as a drug store with a cosmetics section. We carry the prestige lines. Clients understand that they are going to pay a premium for our products. It's no surprise, therefore, that we hear a lot of men say, "You paid *how* much for that?"

This particular week I was working the evening shift. I was helping out my friend and coworker, Debbie, with another line when an elderly gentleman brought his wife to my counter. She was in a wheelchair. I guessed she was in her seventies. She was very beautiful, well put together, and well dressed. Her hair was coifed, her makeup was beautifully applied, and her overall appearance was simply immaculate.

Her husband wheeled her over to me and she said, "Excuse me, ma'am. I'm looking for some eye shadows. I would like to try some new colors and some new lipsticks, too. Do you think you could help me?"

She was such a sweet lady. I took one look at her and replied, "Of course! Please come over here."

Her husband followed me wheeling her to the product display areas. "Would you allow me to apply some eye shadow on you?"

When she replied to me this time, I noticed a quiver in her voice. "Yes, please do." I don't know exactly what illness she had, but I could clearly see that her hands were trembling.

"What's your name, ma'am?"

"Karen."

"Well, Miss Karen, may I remove the eye makeup you have on now so that we can try some new colors?"

Karen looked up at me and said, "You have such beautiful eyes. What are you wearing?" I showed her the colors that I was wearing that night. "I'd like to try those!"

"Okay." I proceeded to remove her existing eye makeup before starting to apply the new shadows. As we were talking, she was not only telling me about the skin care and makeup products she currently uses, but also asking me very detailed questions. She was very knowledgeable about the line and the use of sophisticated makeup techniques.

While she and I were talking, I noticed that her husband was standing to the side and studiously watching everything I was doing. He never interfered or commented. This was not typical when a husband and wife approached the cosmetics counter together. I was not used to a man standing over my shoulder while I was doing a makeover. When a woman comes to us accompanied by a man, he usually finds one of the chairs around the department and sits there impatiently waiting for her to finish. Or, he would wander off to another department for a while and then come back earnestly hoping she was ready. I hardly ever see a man stay nearby and watch intently while I am doing a makeover.

I put the colors on one of Karen's eye just to see how she liked it, thinking I could change it up until she found a combination she liked. Then I would make the other eye match when she made her choice. When we were finished, she looked at her husband and asked, "What do you think, Sweetie?"

"Oh! I love the purple. It makes your eyes *pop*!"

His response was so funny to me, because that is typically a female response. Everyone wants eye shadows that are dramatic and accentuate the color of the eyes. When a woman finds the right color eye shadow, she frequently uses the term "pop" to describe the effect. I almost wanted to laugh hearing a man use that term. As I looked at him again, he was still standing there with his arms crossed, intensely listening and watching. Then something inside me realized that he must have a purpose for paying such close attention.

When I finished the makeover, Karen chose the colors she wanted. I asked her to follow me to the terminal so that she could make her payment. I rang up her purchases and turned to her saying, "Ma'am, how would you like to pay for this?"

Before she answered me, she turned to her husband and gave him a brief nod. On her signal, he moved into position and lifted her out of the wheelchair so that she could stand at the counter. He handed her purse to her, but she took charge of completing the transaction from there. She opened her purse by herself, and then took out her wallet by herself. Because of the trembling, everything was an effort for her. Next she zipped open her wallet, took out her credit card and did the swipe. Even though these were mundane tasks, they took more time than usual because of her trembling.

We stood there while she struggled to complete each step in the process. All the while, Karen's husband was standing behind her with his hands on her waist, half holding her and half gently pushing her toward the counter to brace her. She signed the terminal by herself, and then she decided she wanted something else.

"Oh, I forgot. I need something else. Would you go get this lipstick for me as well, dear?" From her purse, she pulled out a tube that was almost completely gone.

"Yes ma'am. I'd be happy to get that for you," I said. When I came back, we had to go through the entire purchase process again. She was standing there the whole time. Her husband never once got into her purse. He never once said to her, "Oh, let me do that for you." Clearly he was honoring her desire to be as independent as she could be.

It was also clear that because of her tremors, there was no way she was going to put on makeup the way she was made up, particularly eyeliner and lip liner. She was completely made up. Eyeliner, mascara, lip liner, everything. Somebody had to take the time to do that for her. There was no way she could put on eyeliner with any precision the way she was constantly trembling. That's why her husband was standing over there watching. He was watching what I was doing because he was the one who would do it for her later.

The exchange between the two of them was impressively loving and sweet. What I saw in this man was such obvious love for his wife. He cared for her. I don't know if Karen had Parkinson's, but clearly it was debilitating. It didn't matter. When he looked at her, he was so expressive in his admiration for her as a woman.

When we finished, Karen looked at me, and said, "Peggy, thank you so much."

"No ma'am, it was my pleasure. I hope you enjoy everything." Then her husband thanked me also, and the two of them turned to go on their way together. Looking at them, I just knew they had a special love. I heard the Lord saying to me, "That's how attentive I am to you." The Scriptures talk about the different kinds of love. There is erotic love, which is a sexual love. There is fileo, which is the love you would have for a friend. Then there is agape love. This was my second opportunity to witness the manifestation of agape love between two people. Their interaction with each other was a blessing to me. I got to see two people in a marriage living their vows, "...for better or worse, in sickness and in health..." In this case, you could tell there was a love, an affection, an appreciation, a respect between the two of them. He was there to take up the slack for her when she needed help with simple tasks. At the same time, he respected her desire to do as much as she could on her own, as a consummate gentleman would always do.

It's funny. I work in a department where what I sell is mostly about vanity. Let's face it. Nobody *needs* to buy a $30 mascara, or a $60 foundation. The people that buy high-end cosmetics for the color are women who want to invest in the way they look. It was interesting to watch this couple because it was clear that Karen cared about taking care of herself and being the best she could be without limiting herself based on her circumstances. It was also clear that someone else's love was helping her to look that way. That is the way that God loves us. That is the attention that He pays to us. God cares about the most minor things. We often forget that this is how God loves us. If we could see in the spirit the way that God loves us, it would look like the way that Karen's husband loves her.

Scripture defines the Holy Spirit as the "Devine Paraclete". *Paraclitos* in Greek, refers to 'something inside you', something that sticks. It is a parasite. It never leaves you. This is what the Holy Spirit is - the divine parasite. The Holy Spirit, however, is also a gentleman. He never intrudes on anyone. He is there to support, encourage, and edify, but He is no enabler. In this fallen world, we may face challenges that sap our strength and impede our progress, but His power will be there to help us to rise to any occasion. He binds us to the love of God. As the Word says, *"For I am convinced that neither death nor life, neither angels nor demons, neither the present nor the future, nor any powers, neither height nor depth, nor anything else in all creation, will be able to separate us from the love of God that is in Christ Jesus our Lord"* (NIV: Romans 8:38-39).

That is what I saw in this man's eyes for his wife. You can't fake it. How often do we see one partner abandon the other in circumstances like this? Not all men do this, but there are a lot of single mothers out there that are suffering the painful consequences of abandonment. Every married couple starts out by saying the words, "for better or worse", I'm sticking. I'm not going anywhere. The relationship that Karen has with her husband is the essence of a loving commitment. This is how it looks when you make a commitment. He does not make her feel less human or unworthy of love because he has to hold her against the counter so she can stand. The covenant marriage commitment does not endure solely on the eros or fileo kind of love. A long-term marriage endures with agape love. Agape means I choose to let the love of God flow through me to my partner. It is a surrender of my will. It is a beautiful thing to see.

In my generation, the divorce rate for first marriages hovers around 25%, and the divorce rate for second marriages is even higher. Even some members of the church have not set a good example in many cases where the divorce rate is also high. The consequence is that many of our children have never seen an example of a strong marriage commitment between their parents. The question has to be, what's the problem? Why? Well, perhaps we think that love is a feeling. My mother used to say, "When you've lost those lovin' feelings, you'd better get down on your knees and figure out a way to get them back." Loving someone requires a decision to remain faithful. It is based on a commitment to God. It's a choice to honor God, then to honor your spouse. You stay because you are asking God to give you a love for your spouse that is not based on circumstances. It is not of the flesh. It is a spiritual act.

The relationship between Karen and her husband was a beautiful thing to see. They were there to make a purchase. I was just the makeup consultant at the counter. They had no idea they were making a profound impression on me.

I went over to my friend Debbie and said, "Now that's the way it is supposed to look." Many women never get to experience this kind of love. Women are so often devalued and give themselves away for nothing. They don't have a picture of agape love. I wished I had a video camera with me that evening so that I could have played it for my daughters and said to them, "Look at this. Do you see this?" When you get married, you are not getting married for lust. You're getting married to someone who will love you in both the good times and the bad. If the unexpected should happen and life puts you in a wheelchair, you want to have a man that's going to say to you, "Not only are you going to go out with me in a wheelchair, but I'm going to do my best to make sure that you are the classiest woman in the room." That's a relationship that reflects the heart of God.

Dear Daddy, thank You for showing us how You love. The world gives us such distorted pictures of love in the media. Marriage is not just a contract. It is a covenant that You instituted as a way to demonstrate the spiritual intimacy You desire with each of us. We are the recipients of such extravagant love from You.

We live in a fallen world, where people will "try one another", as though they were shopping for clothes. We keep it until it is out of style or no longer fits. Even in the church, we have drifted so far from You that we lack a true understanding of a covenant relationship. We make lofty promises on wedding days and forget too soon that we stood before You to make vows for which we will answer one day.

I pray for my marriage. Draw my spouse and me close to You. Teach us how to be one in You without sacrificing our individuality. Teach us to pray together and seek Your face about everything that concerns us. Help us to understand that we have an adversary that wants to tear us completely apart. Forgive us for where we have failed You, failed each other, and failed the society around us. Help us to grow up spiritually. We cannot do this without You, but we can do all things through You.

For anyone contemplating divorce, I ask that You would intervene on their behalf. Convict and convince each of them about their own sin. You are the Righteous Judge. Soften their hearts. Help them to consider the life-altering consequences to everyone around them, especially their children. Heal the wounds they have inflicted on each other. Help them to understand that there are some things worth fighting to keep.

For those who have suffered from a painful divorce, give them hope to believe in life and love again. Help them to see that their life is not over. Ease their pain. Restore their self-confidence. Show them their future. Help them not to repeat the mistakes of the past.

For those that are single, show them an example of genuine love between a man and a woman - your kind of love. They may not have ever known You as a role model. Help them not to make decisions because they have confused lust with love. Help them to hear Your voice about the mate they choose. You expect marriage to be for life. You expect us to honor our commitment.

In Jesus' name, so be it! Amen.

Makeup Lesson 17: Lip Color and Treatment

($) Your smile is one of the first attributes that people notice about you. A woman enhances this important feature by the way she accents her lips with color. The **Minimalist** will generally lean toward more neutral shades of lip color, or possibly only use a light neutral gloss. She will stay away from bright colors. If she uses color at all, it will be in warm tones. The **Classic** will use colors which may be rich in either warm or cool shades, and may follow with a pale lip gloss as a top coat. The **Dramatic** will not be afraid of trendy bright reds or violets, followed by very shiny gloss. The **Classic** and the **Dramatic** will use lip liner as well.

Whatever your personal style, the objective should be to enhance the lips and pull the whole look together. For instance, you want to choose blush color and eye shadows that are in the same color palate as the lip color. As with any makeup, the look should be consistent and tastefully applied.

Lip liners come in corresponding shades to lip colors. I find that the best are waterproof and can be removed with cleanser. Lip liner can embellish the lips by making them appear fuller, or just outlining them to give the lips a more defined appearance. Trends will change. In current trends, the liner closely corresponds to the natural shade of the lip.

Pay attention to what is known as the bow of the lip. Gently outline the "V" in the middle of your mouth and then gradually work your way down to the corners of each side with small dash strokes. The best lip liners will have a brush or a paddle on the opposite end. Use these tools to apply your lip color and then blend the liner with it as well.

Having a tendency to have a dry mouth, I always wear lip gloss over lip color. This helps me keep my lips moist. There is a product called Lip Fix. This creates a smooth foundation for lip color and assists with "feathering" that can occur. Other products will treat lips which are consistently dry or chapped due to climate or medications. If you use these products first, it will assist you in the smooth application of the products to follow.

Use lip treatments at night while you sleep. Lips are tender skin and need to be protected and nourished. Instead of using your hand, test lip colors on your fingertips where the color of the skin most closely matches the color of your lips.

Lesson #18

Let God Bless You

One night I was working the late shift with Holly, who had just been named the manager for the elite cosmetics line. I was standing at my counter when she came up to me and said, "I understand that you pray for people."

I smiled and said, "Yes, I do."

"Would you please pray for me?" she asked with a clear tone of desperation.

"What's wrong, Holly?"

"My stepfather died last night. He and my mother live in Washington state, and I'm here in Dallas. And, um, I don't have the money to go home for the funeral. It's too expensive. So I can't go." She paused for a moment and continued, "I think I'm going to be made the counter manager here. Technically speaking, I've been the acting manager for the last five or six days. They haven't told me officially that I have the position, so I don't know exactly. Somebody has to do the manager's job. I don't feel comfortable calling in a vacation request because there's no one else here to cover for me. And, if I am being considered for the job, then I can't request vacation time right now.

"On top of all that, I'm in the middle of a custody battle over my daughter with my ex-husband. I have to put down $2,500 from my savings to retain an attorney. It's money that I really don't have. I'm here, and I'm working, and I'm just trying to get through the day."

I said, "Absolutely I will pray for you." We walked over to her bay, and I began to pray for her.

> *"Father, You said we could come boldly to Your throne of grace. Holly is in a very, very difficult place emotionally and psychologically. She needs You right now. I am asking You on her behalf to show up as only You can do. I pray protection over her. I pray the peace of God over her. I pray the bloodline circle of Jesus around her and her daughter. I forbid the enemy from crossing over that bloodline. I pray that You would deal with Holly's ex-husband by speaking to him in dreams and visions. I pray that You would comfort Holly and her family."*

As I finished, Holly dried her eyes. I hugged her and asked her, "When is your court date?"

"Two weeks from Thursday."

"I'll pray for you that day."

Holly was astonished. "You'll do that for me?"

"Yes, I will. People did that for me when I went through my divorce. They stood with me. I know how it feels to be so frightened that you want to vomit. You are not alone. That's why I'm here. God wants you to know that you are never alone."

She thanked me and I went back to my work. We were both scheduled to work until 10 p.m. As the end our shift approached, I walked over to Holly and said, "I'm going to give you my cell phone number. I want you to call or text me. You don't have to give me a lot of specific details, but if there is something you want me to pray for, I will pray for you."

Holly was genuinely moved and surprised that I would stop what I was doing at work and pray for her right in the middle of MDS. I told her, "Well, sweetie, I have made a personal commitment to pray for people when they ask me. I understand that most people will say yes to anyone who asks for prayer without ever doing it. They easily forget if they don't pray right then and there. In a crisis, however, that is exactly what they need to do. They need to stop and do the only thing that matters."

Often when we get hit or blind-sided by events, we will try to do whatever we can to fix it. Then when there is no other way a situation can be fixed, we throw up our hands and say, "Well, I guess there's nothing else we can do but pray." Isn't it ridiculous that, in a crisis, the first thing we should be doing is the last thing we finally do? If we would reverse our approach by praying first, how many of our struggles could we eliminate, or at least make more manageable? Instead, we wait until we are in over our heads, and then expect God to ride in on His white horse and do major damage control. Sometimes, God does ride in on a white horse. Although I wonder in my own life if everything had to be as hard for me in the cleanup phase. I believe there were some things I could have avoided simply by seeking His counsel and getting a Rhema word before I set out to do things my way.

I told Holly about a book I owned that was filled with anointed prayers. "Holly, this book was important to me for two reasons. First, each prayer is focused on a common human experience and is composed using God's Word. Through this book, I learned to pray according to the will of God, which everyone can discover through His Word: *'And this is the confidence which we have in Him: We are sure that if we ask anything according to His will, He listens to and hears us. And if we positively know that He listens to us in whatever we ask, we also know with settled and absolute knowledge that we have granted us as our present possessions the requests made of Him'* (1 John 5:14-15). Second, Holly, I learned to pray believing that I will receive what I request. *'For this reason I am telling you, whatever you ask for in prayer, believe, trust, and be confident that it is granted to you, and you will get it'* (Mark 11:24). This book taught me how to pray the Word of God. The more I prayed, the easier it became for me to believe Him."

I shared my testimony with Holly and explained to her, "About twelve years ago I was in a situation that looked very similar to the place where you are right now. I was a single mother, completely overwhelmed. Was that a bad place? Yes, it was a horrible place! Looking back, though, when I cried out to God, He answered me. He gave me a strategy."

Holly started to give me the background to her story. She said, "My divorce was mutual. We both wanted it. I'm not saying anything bad about my ex, but there were things going on that I believed I could no longer live with, and the love I felt for him was destroyed. Because it was mutual, we were able to decide to get along for the sake of our Angel, which is my nickname for my daughter. For the first year, everything went pretty well until he got involved with another woman who had a child. That's when our relationship started to go south.

"As for me, it has been five years now and I've never grieved my divorce. I just made up my mind that I'm not going to become involved with a man because I'm too afraid that I might choose poorly, and I don't want to inflict that pain on my Angel. So, my Angel has become my life. When it comes to dating, I just don't go there."

I thought to myself how sweet it was that Holly called her daughter her "Angel". The daughter has another given name, but whenever Holly spoke to or about her she used the nickname "Angel". In Holly's life, her daughter was her angel. I told Holly, "I think it's beautiful that you call your daughter 'Angel', because every time you pronounce that over your child, you are confirming to her what you believe she is."

Then I looked at Holly and said, "I understand what you're saying, but did it ever occur to you that God might just bring a spirit-filled, godly man into your life to be a guardian angel to Angel? If you are saying now that she feels rejected by her natural father, or at best he sweeps into and out of her life, did it ever occur to you that God would bring someone into your life to bless you and in turn be a blessing to your daughter?"

Holly looked me as though that thought had never occurred to her. She just stared at me and began to cry. "Holly, you are a beautiful woman. Do you not think that you are worthy of a right relationship, of a godly relationship? Do you not think that God would allow you to have that?"

Crying, Holly responded, "I am very afraid. I have been afraid for so long that I am tired of being afraid."

"I understand how that feels, Holly. I can't say that you will never be hurt again, but I do believe that you will be safe if God is in the relationship with you because He says, '*When you pass through the waters, I will be with you, and through the rivers, they will not overwhelm you. When you walk through the fire, you will not be burned or scorched ...*' (Isaiah 43:2).

"God loves you, Holly. He has promised to give you an abundant life (John 10:10). I believe He intends for us to have a life filled with love. Now I am not saying that God is going to give you this kind of a relationship in the next month, or even in the next ten years by the time that Angel turns 18. I don't know what God is going to do, but I believe that if God is not going to give you a loving, intimate relationship in your life, then He will give you grace to live fulfilled without it.

"Did it ever occur to you though, that He may have a plan for your life that includes a loving relationship with a man? You are presupposing His will by shutting that part of your life off, not because God said this is His will for you, but because you are afraid. That doesn't make sense to me. Ask God for what you would like. Seek His will. Don't just deliberately shut yourself off to love and to your feelings. You have shut down emotionally. I can't believe that is healthy or right."

Holly was softly weeping. I reached out to her. Of course, by this time it was late and there was no one in the store. I just wrapped my arms around her and I asked,

> *"Father, please bring this woman a love note. Father, please minister to my friend. Wrap her up in Your arms and show her the value she has as Your daughter. Let her see herself through Your eyes. This woman has been stripped by fear to the point where she denies the desires of her heart. Lord, give her the strength tonight to open herself up to feel and to receive love."*

Holly thanked me profusely for praying for her. We said good night, and I left work to go home. When I came back to work the next day, I saw Holly. Her countenance was completely peaceful, bright, and happy! She was beaming.

"Girl, you look good today!" I gushed.

Holly stopped and said, "Thank you so much for praying for me last night. I felt that!"

"What you are experiencing, Holly, is the love of God pouring the truth into you. The Word says we are washed with the water of the Word (Ephesians 5:26). When the Word comes into you, you are washed clean of all those misconceptions, preconceived ideas, heartache, and pain. The Lord is washing that dirt and debris that is sticking to you. You programmed yourself to believe all that negativity, but it is not the truth. When someone speaks the truth of the Word of God over you, it washes you. The true Word purges and cleanses you.

Holly was looking at me, and she started to apologize to me. "Peggy, I owe you an apology."

"For what?"

"I just want to tell you that I'm sorry that I didn't understand you when you first came to work here." Then she said, "You are a gorgeous woman. When you first came here I thought that you were just so beautiful, but I thought you seemed aloof. We didn't know you very well and didn't know what to do with you."

"I'm sorry that you felt that way," I responded. "The truth is that I went through a very difficult year in 2011. I experienced huge betrayal, both personal and in business. I was coming back to work here to earn just enough money to pay my basic bills and get my legs underneath me. I needed to find out just exactly what God wanted me to do with the rest of my life. I believed I had started a project that God wanted me to do. There was no funding for it, however, and I had to make a living. I was questioning where I was supposed to be, and how was I supposed to process what had happened to me?

"When I started working here, I also felt as though you three had a rhythm based on working together for years. I felt as though I didn't belong and didn't know how things were supposed to work. I was only here to make a living and try to do a good job, but I didn't feel accepted by the team when I worked on this line.

"Then when I went to work on my current line, I just backed away from you. I didn't feel the need to compete or arm wrestle people over commissions. I continued to ask God to reveal my purpose here. 'Father, is this the wrong place for me to be? Should I quit? Should I go find something else?' I stayed here because it gave me the schedule flexibility I wanted, which a regular 9-5 job wouldn't give me. So I decided yes, this was where the Lord wanted me, and I made a decision to be thankful for my job and try to live peaceably with everybody."

Then I started to share with Holly the story of the woman who couldn't decide which blush color she wanted. "That precious woman broke into tears and told me that she couldn't make up her mind because she was on her way to find long-term care for her forty-six year old daughter who was in a permanent coma. Compared to finding a nursing home, finding the right blush was low on her list of priorities."

Holly was looking at me, and her eyes were filling up with tears. "After I helped the woman, I said to her, 'Did it ever occur to you that God sent you to this counter to me because I am a believer, and I was going to be the one to tell you that if God cared enough to send you to someone who is going to help you pick out a blush, then surely He was not going to abandon you when you need to find a nursing home for your daughter?'"

I said, "From that moment on, there was a shift in me. I began to see with spiritual eyes, and the Lord began to speak to me. He said, 'Peggy, believe that I am going to do your passion project, "In Search of Steel Magnolias". If I put you in the cosmetics department, just for a while, will you trust me and be obedient?' My response was, 'Yes, Father.' Holly, He already knew that you would see this day when you would need to know that you are not alone. Even though you have no family with you, you have sisters in Christ whom He has strategically placed around you to pray for you and comfort you. God has been mindful of you all along."

Holly was wiping tears away as I continued, "Holly, I have many experiences like this. Many times I come to work and these things happen so frequently that I have come to expect it. I'm here and I feel like a magnet. God brings these people to my little cosmetics bay, and He is teaching me that He values success differently than man does. Success to Him is me doing what He says that I'm supposed to do and being what He says that I'm supposed to be. The definition of success has new meaning to me.

"What if I had left, Holly? What if I had given into the thoughts that I don't belong here; that no one likes me here? What if I had allowed other people to define me? Even though I wasn't always comfortable here, I realized that your definition of me, or rejection of me, had nothing to do with me as a person. I am who God tells me I am, and I go where He tells me to go, whether I am comfortable or not. I am on assignment.

"I remember the one time around Christmas my feet were hurting after work. Since getting this job, I have been in a constant pursuit of comfortable shoes. I was awake in the middle of the night because my legs were cramping so badly. I was lying in bed crying out to the Lord, 'Jesus, You want me to be here, and I see that I am being a blessing, but my feet hurt.' I heard an answer in my spirit, 'Yes, I know how that feels. There was a time when My feet hurt, too.' So I thought of Jesus on the cross with nails in His feet. I didn't feel condemned when He said this to me. I just laughed out loud in the middle of the night because it seemed so ludicrous for me to be complaining about my feet when He did what the Father told Him to do. I found myself saying, 'Okay, Lord, I guess I'm not going to be complaining about my feet anymore!' And I never did after that, because I understood that this was a small price to pay for the privilege of being His servant.

"When I started coming to work, Holly, my focus wasn't on commissions anymore. Suddenly, I started to see God do amazing things with the development of "In Search of Steel Magnolias". First, there was a website. Then there were t-shirts, and a trailer. The Lord was taking care of that business for me. It is not that I wasn't trying to pursue it. I just wasn't sweating over it. I wasn't anxious about it. I wasn't trying to force things to happen. Everything was unfolding while I obediently stayed where He told me to be. God was teaching me that we are the Kingdom of God on earth. We embody Christ. We are His arms, His feet, and His voice. That means whenever we show up, He shows up. We may think we are in certain situations for one reason, but actually our purpose is to transact Kingdom business. We have to be enlightened to think with a Kingdom mentality, or we will miss the opportunities that are around us every day.

"So I'm thinking to myself that I have known the Lord for fifty years. Only in the last year of my life, however, have I ever experienced anything quite like this. What is this? I felt the Lord say to me, 'I have shifted your perspective, and now you hear My instructions. You are alert and looking for the opportunities I present. You are willing and obedient to act; therefore, I will send people to you. You are not looking to this job as your total means of support. I am your source. You go where I want you to go. I'll take care of your support.'"

I told this to Holly and said, "I felt my joy starting to come back. The joy of the Lord, Holly, is your strength as well." Holly was looking at me still crying, but smiling and laughing at the same time. I knew that feeling. I knew how it felt when God starts talking to you. It's resonating, and it's breaking you, but you're laughing and there is joy, and it's all happening at the same time.

Holly was wiping her eyes, and she was saying over and over to me, "Thank you. Thank you, Peggy. I have felt so alone."

"Well, you're not. I'm going to go one step further, actually two steps further with you, if you will let me. This is just…you don't have to do this."

"Well, what is it?"

"You told me that your court date is October fourth, right?"

"That's right."

"Would you like me to come to court with you?"

Her mouth dropped. "You would come to court with me?"

"Absolutely, I'll go. I don't need to get in your business. Your ex doesn't even need to know that I'm with you. I'll show up wherever it is and sit in the corner. For all he'll know, I'll just be another person going to court. I'll sit there praying silently from my prayer book. He won't know, but you'll know that there is another believer in there praying for you. I will also fast that day for you."

Holly was stunned and speechless. "You would fast for me?"

"Yes! Holly, that's what happened for me when I went through my divorce with my first husband. Several women showed up for me at court. They fasted for me. They did not get in my business, but they showed up. When I walked into court, I knew that my ex-husband thought that I was alone, but I knew that I wasn't. If you want me to be there, then I will go."

Holly shook her head and looked at me as though I was from Mars.

"I know how it feels to be alone. I was an only child. When I went through the trauma of my divorce, I felt completely vulnerable with no physical and very little emotional support from extended family members. Yes, I had my mother and aunt, but they were both ill and frightened. My lawyer was my support, but other believers also stood in the gap for me. All I'm going to do is stand in the gap for you. Sometimes when people know someone is in trouble, they may not pray because they feel inhibited. Even though we're at work, we have prayed together twice tonight, haven't we? There's no reason we can't pray together. People who may see us are simply going to think we are standing here talking. It's not jeopardizing our jobs, and we are taking care of Kingdom business right now."

I continued sharing with her how I prayed my way through things. "I have found that the most horrible experiences in my life have stopped me from looking at people as my anchor and driven me instead toward God. I discovered through my sorrow that God was enough. When I needed Jesus with some skin on, He would send people to me to give me comfort. Ultimately, He was the source. They were just conduits of His grace. I come to work now, Holly, and I am always anticipating what God is going to do. I never know what it's going to be, but I just show up and say, 'Father, I'm willing. Whatever it is, I'm here.'

"Holly, God wants me here right now so that you know that He has never left you. He knows that you need arms to hold you, which brings us back to you shutting yourself off from love. Holly, you are a beautiful woman and God has great things ahead for you."

I hugged her again and went back to my counter to take care of a client. A little later, I heard her laughing and laughing over at her counter, which was quite different from the woman who was crying buckets and felt lost and vulnerable just the night before. After I had finished with my client, I tiptoed over to her counter and saw her with a man buying serum for the eyes. They were cutting up and laughing hysterically. Debbie was also with her giggling, and together they looked like school girls.

"Do I hear some major flirting going on over there?"

Debbie said, "Holly was talking to this guy about skincare. He was absolutely, totally infatuated with her."

Holly was glowing. She looked at Debbie and said, "Peggy prayed for me! Peggy prayed for me last night."

Holly then looked at me and said, "Peggy, I know that man is a client, but the fear is gone. The fear of allowing myself to be appreciated by someone is gone. That's all that was. He wasn't weird or some freak, just a sweet gentleman. He was cute, too. When I gave him his purchases, he turned around and said to me, 'You got me so shaken up, I forgot which way I came in.' We both laughed, and he was blushing."

If I didn't know better, I would have bet that somebody overheard our conversation and set her up with this experience. Holly was looking at me and said to me, "You know what? My heart is pounding… in a good way. It's nice to feel this way. It's nice to …"

I finished her sentence, "…feel like a woman. Feel like somebody notices you for the lovely woman you are. It's nice, isn't it? That's who you are, Holly. It may have been happening all along, but you were not open to it. Do you remember that I asked God to give you a love note? Well, there you have it. It's not as though you two are going to run out and jump in the sack or do something stupid. He may come back around or he may not. That's not the point. The point is that you are a smart, beautiful and multifaceted gem of a woman. You are not just a mother. Being a mother is wonderful, but that is not all that you are. You have chosen, however, to see yourself only in that role, and you were not going to let any man come around because you had a bad experience. You numbed your feelings.

"I used to numb my feelings, too, when I was so caught up taking care of everyone else in my family. I remember when I had just started dating my current husband, Jim. It was a cold December day, and Jim came over to visit. When I answered the door barefooted, he took one look at me and abruptly said, 'Where are your socks? Go get your socks on!' I was so startled that I couldn't say anything. I just turned and went to my bedroom closet muttering to myself about how rude he was. He never even said hello. I was on the floor looking for my slippers and feeling a bit miffed, when I noticed for the first time that my feet were freezing. I sat on the closet floor and began to weep. I was so out of touch with myself rushing to take care of everyone else, that I never noticed how cold my feet were. I needed someone else to tell me.

"What's happening to you, Holly, is that you are thawing. You froze yourself by an act of will, and now you're thawing. Now, just be open to God's blessing for your life and let God bring love into it. He will let you know what is from Him and what is not."

As I looked at Holly, she was beaming, grinning from ear to ear. Debbie was standing nearby, listening. She had been in the same frame of mind as Holly with respect to relationships with men. "You know what I would like the two of you to do?"

"What?" they echoed.

"Why don't both of you go home and take a bubble bath. Relax and have some quiet time. Write what you would want if you were to have the relationship of your dreams. I got the biggest surprise when I realized that God is nice. It changed my whole outlook. I think what is happening to the two of you now is what has already happened to me. Subconsciously, you have made God out to be just like the men you have known. God is nothing like them. He is the consummate gentleman. He loves you unconditionally. If He loves you enough to have given Jesus to die for you, then what does that mean? Is He going to save you so that you don't go to hell, but while you're here on earth, it feels like hell and a crapshoot? That doesn't make sense. Don't you think He understands your human need for relationship and intimacy? Don't you think He knows?

"Holly, you love Angel. She is the love of your life, right?"

"Yes."

"What happens at Christmas?"

"What do you mean?"

"Well, don't you ask her for a list?"

"Y..Yeah."

"What do you say to her? You say, 'What would you like for Christmas?' Christmas is not about giving her a toothbrush and toothpaste and deodorant and the necessities. Christmas is a celebration where you give your loved ones extravagant gifts, or the best you can give. The Bible says, '...

you do not have, because you do not ask' (James 4:2)."

Both Debbie and Holly were staring at me as though I was an alien. I can see in their expressions that this concept had never registered with them. "Did it ever occur to you that God would be that nice? The Word says, *'For God so greatly loved and dearly prized the world that He even gave up His only begotten Son, so that whoever believes in Him shall not perish but have eternal life'* (John 3:16). If God loves you that much to have sent Jesus, then He also knows you have basic human needs for love, affection, warmth, and provision. Do you think He would withhold that from you, but give you eternal life?

"Go home and think about what you want and write it down. Do you even know what you want, or have you had too much heartache to know? Have you ever thought about it, or do you expect life just to happen? When a new relationship looks as though it has potential, are your first thoughts, *Just don't hurt me,* and *How do I protect myself?* Have you ever asked God to bring to you what He wants for you, and what would complete you? What do you think He would do if you did?"

Now Debbie and Holly were laughing and smiling. The night before with Holly was like injecting her with spiritual morphine. Today I injected them both with hope for the future and the joy of the Lord, and they responded. Less than twenty-four hours later, God confirmed it. He caused a circumstance to validate everything I said to Holly. This accomplished two things. First, God proved Himself to her. I asked God to affirm her, and He gave her a love note. Second, she was beginning to understand the power of prayer. Out of her mouth she recognized this power when she said, "Peggy prayed for me!"

I continued, "You shouldn't spend your life grieving or presume your future by saying, 'Oh, well, my life is not what I expected. All my relationships have ended painfully, so I'm just going to assume the worst is always going to happen. Then, I won't be surprised when I get hurt.'

"Instead, start expecting the best. Believe that God loves you. Spend time with Him and get to know Him. When you do, you will find out that He wants to give you joy. He wants you to be fulfilled. Joy will always be in the center of His will. If He wants you to live your life as a single person and there is purpose, then He is going to give you a desire and grace for that. You are not going to make life choices out of fear."

So I just hugged Holly, and she told me, "Thank you! Thank you! Thank you!" And she was laughing.

We were close to closing time, so I went to take a quick break. When I came back, I noticed that the two of them had already gone up to deliver their cash envelopes to the management office. While I was going upstairs on the escalator to deliver mine, I saw them coming down the escalator. Again, I heard Holly laughing (she has a very distinct laugh). Evidently something was going on. So I said, "Hey, Holly!"

"What?"

"It's great to hear that laugh!" and I blew her a kiss and mouthed the words, "I love you!"

She blew me a kiss back and said, "I love you, too", and continued laughing. The woman who was bawling her eyes out the night before was now laughing hysterically. She had slammed the door shut on her feelings and would not give herself permission to feel. Now, something inside her broke open. It was the joy of the Lord.

The dangerous thing about slamming the door to feeling the negative, painful emotions is that you do not get to embrace fully the loving, positive ones, either. When I shut down emotionally, I often shut down both the good and the bad feelings. I do not think that God wants me to live that way. I do not believe He wants me to remain an emotional victim of someone else's poor choices, or my own. He doesn't want me to be trapped in emotional bondage from the past. When I experience a great loss, I need to complete the grieving process and move forward.

My mother was emotionally trapped after my father's death. As a matter of fact, when my mother died, she told me that she believed her life had purpose when we were in ministry with him. Well, his ministry ended in 1973 when he died, and she did not die until 2003 - thirty years later! She told herself that there would never be another man like my father, which was probably true as he was unusually gifted. It doesn't mean, however, that she could not have experienced a love with someone else that could have been just as rich and fulfilling in a different way. I don't believe she ever allowed herself to consider that possibility.

Plus, she had gained so much weight. They fell in love with each other when they were both young and beautiful. Then he got heavy and sick. She also got heavy and convinced herself that no one would ever want her. I remember once my father telling me that when he went to be with the Lord, he hoped my mother would find a loving man to be good to her and take care of her. She was self-conscious, so she put herself in a box, and ended up living her life vicariously through me. I just wanted her to pursue the dreams that were in her heart.

My mother said she always wanted to be an English teacher. She was smart, intuitive, and an excellent speaker who knew the Word. She sat under my father's ministry for years and could have been a speaker similar to Beth Moore. She wrote poetry and lyrics to songs. She had the best sense of humor and an incredible amount of wisdom. She was always gracious and generous, and contributed so much to so many people. She never saw herself, however, as anything but a supportive partner for my father, then subsequently for me, both in my ministry, my professional work, and then in my role as a mother. While I am grateful for every loving act of support from her, I have some personal regret that she placed limitations on herself. What potential goes unrealized when we define ourselves by our past, or feel inhibited by our current circumstances? God inside of us is big enough to carry us forward. Still, I am proud of what my mother was able to contribute in her life and the strength in Christ she exhibited dealing with her own horrible terminal illness.

In Holly's case, I think she responded when I spoke a different truth into her spirit. I simply expressed a higher potential for her life. Through prayer, she became open to a new possibility, and God blessed her with affirmation. When I told Holly that I would go to court with her, just as other women had done the same for me years ago, she recognized that she did not have to carry her burdens alone. She was now willing to build connections instead of walls. This is what we as the body of Christ are supposed to be doing for each other.

Even though I was exhausted from working a long day, I walked to my car that night feeling elated. Twenty-four hours after a simple prayer, God dramatically altered Holly's vision for her future from dull to bright. There is purpose to everything that is happening in our lives. Trusting that God has a plan for me is the way I can know that my future can be bright, too. *"For I know the thoughts and plans that I have for you, says the Lord, thoughts and plans for welfare and peace and not for evil, to give you hope in your final outcome"* (Jeremiah 29:11).

Dear Daddy, help me to discern Your perfect will for my life. Help me not to live based on misconceptions or thoughts resulting from my own fears. Thank You that no matter what I have lost, I can begin again. You have the plan. You have the divine calling. You know exactly why You made me and what will fulfill my life.

I call unto You and expect You to answer me and show me great and mighty things hidden from the natural man that I do not know. Reveal Yourself to me. You are eager for my success in every area of my life. You came that I would have an abundant life with You. I have choices. With Your help, I will not remain captive to my failures, losses, mistakes, or poor decisions.

Let me live my life open to love. At the same time, teach me to be discerning about relationships. What may be Your plan for someone else, may not be Your plan for me. I want Your plan. Only You know what is best for me. I submit to Your highest will in my life, and I expect to see You do exceedingly, abundantly above and beyond all that I could ever ask or think.

In Jesus' name, so be it! Amen.

Makeup Lesson 18: Eye Shadows and Liners

($) Minimalists may sweep one shade across the eye lid for a subtle definition. Women who want to create a finished eye shadow look may use three shades: highlight, midtone, and contour. The **highlight shade** is usually the lightest shadow. Everything highlighted will generally come forward. Start by washing the entire eyelid from brow to lash line. Do not forget the inside corner of the lower lash line. This application will help the eyes to appear more open and youthful.

The **mid tone shade** is between the highlight and the contour shades. This should be an extension of your natural skin tone. Change your highlight and contour colors more often than your mid tone shade. To apply, start from the outside corner of the eyelid, because the first place you lay your brush receives the highest concentration of color. Gently move your brush along the crease of the eyelid, from the outside corner to the inside corner.

The **contour shade** is the deepest of the three shades, but not necessarily stark or dark. Because of its depth, your contour shade provides the most dramatic reshaping of your eyelid. To apply, sweep contour color across the top lash line, from the outside corner toward the inside corner. Brushing the shadow along your lash line will help create a blended effect with your eyeliner. Then bring the color up into the outer portion of the crease and blend it inward, about a third or at most halfway across.

Ground rules for **eyeliner**: If you line the bottom lash line, you must line across the top lash line. Without balance the eyes will appear old and tired. The color on the bottom lash line should not be deeper than the color on the top. It will cause the eye to appear to droop. You may line along the top line without lining along the bottom. You do not have to apply eyeliner in one straight, perfect line. Begin at the outside corner of the lower lash line and draw small, featherlike strokes (dashes), connecting each one as you move toward the inside of the eye. Use the same trick on the upper lash line. The inside lash line should have a thinner and less intense application of color than the outside lash line. Apply as close to the roots of the lash as possible with wiggle strokes of the pencil to work the color into the roots. It takes a little practice to become proficient.

Lesson #19

Church of the Holy Lipstick

Because my schedule varied from week to week, my husband often asked me before he left for work, "Are you going to work today?" After each shift, I would come home from work and tell him about these extraordinary encounters praying with my clients and coworkers. Soon my husband, who has his own brand of wry humor, started asking me, "Are you going to the Church of the Holy Lipstick today?"

There were four consultants, including myself, who consistently closed the cosmetics department at the end of each shift. We were developing strong friendships through our close camaraderie. In our group was a woman named Katrina from Croatia. Our team had several employees who were born outside America. One of the reasons I enjoyed working was the opportunity to get to know people from different countries.

Late one evening Diane and I were standing at our bays talking about the Lord. Katrina came up and overheard us talking. Initially, I was not quite sure how she would respond to us. She had always been sweet, and very quiet.

"I know God is real," Katrina interjected.

"You do?"

"I can tell you a story about how I know this."

"Well, please tell us!"

"Many years ago I came to this country with my husband and young son. My husband is a stone cutter. He was commissioned to come to New York City to work on a famous church. When we first arrived in 1991, I had the responsibility to change our money into American dollars. So I left the hotel room and brought my son with me. I knew no English. My son knew a little English, but not enough to help. I thought I knew where to go and what to do, but as soon as I walked out of the hotel onto the street I became intimidated and frightened. New York is a big city. I panicked! Inside, I was screaming, *Oh, God! Oh, God! Oh, God! Oh, God! Oh, God!* I must have said His name a hundred times. I was terrified. I walked and walked with my son until we reached a stoplight. As

I was standing there, I heard two ladies behind me speaking my language. I was shocked! At first, I thought I was in a dream. Someone was speaking Croatian here in New York City. I turned around with tears in my eyes and said to the women, "Please, can you help me? Can you go with me to the bank?" One woman then walked with me to the bank and helped me to exchange money.

"There is no doubt in my mind that God brought those two women to me. He knew I was going to be at that stoplight at that moment. He knew how frightened I was going to be. In the middle of New York among all those millions of people, He prepared a way for me. I know He is real."

Diane and I just stood there. Here we were late at night with nothing to do and we were hearing another testimony of the reality of God. It was easy to see a pattern among each of my friends at work. In each case, there was a crisis moment, followed by prayer, and then God showed up. Even just praying His name could be enough!

I used think that it was silly to think of God this way - God the Rescuer. Then it occurred to me that God is the beginning, the middle, and the end; the alpha and omega (Revelation 22:13). He has seen time completed. God already knew each one of us from the foundations of the earth. He has already seen our crisis moments and orchestrated a solution.

Escape is different from rescue. When we escape, we *do* something. When we are rescued, something is *done* for us. There have been several times in my life when I knew I was in danger. I could not save myself. There was nothing I could do. Just prior to one of the most serious situations in my life, I was listening to Bishop T.D. Jakes. He described how we may be faced with circumstances in our lives where we are held captive and totally helpless. That's when we need "Rambo God". This is the God who knows where you are being held, and intervenes to get you out. Then like Rambo, He slaps some black paint on His face, wraps a bandana around His head, puts a knife in His teeth and says, "Sit tight, baby, I coming to get you!"

Little did I know that soon I would be crying out for "Rambo God". He heard me. He was faithful. He always is! God came to Katrina's rescue on a street corner in New York City. He has come for me. He will come for you. Why do we wait so long to cry out to Him? Even death is the ultimate rescue operation. Through salvation, we no longer have to fear death, for God has made a way to rescue us, through His son, Jesus.

In Katrina's case, God already knew she was going to cry out to Him. Even before she knew she would cry out, He arranged for those two ladies who spoke Croatian to show up. What a compassionate, amazing, intimate God! No one else heard Katrina crying out. She was screaming inside her spirit. She was in a strange city with a small child and no one to help but God.

Have you ever been screaming on the inside? Have you ever cried yourself to sleep, agonizing over situations or secrets that no one else knew? God hears you! He cares! You are not alone. I know this. He has heard me.

Mary was another woman in our small group. She also started in the fragrance department and soon came downstairs to work in one of the prestige lines. Mary was from Louisiana and had a very sharp wit. She happened to hear us talking on another night before closing, and she volunteered to share her testimony, which she recently gave in her own church.

"I had two big issues in my life. My first issue was that I was a smoker since I was fourteen. I wanted to quit. I tried to quit so many times, but never could. My second issue was my younger sister. We viciously hated each other growing up. She did and said some horribly cruel things to me when we lived in my parents' home. Our relationship never improved when we became adults. I could not forgive her, and the way she continued to treat me made me feel justified in hating her. Every time she would say something to hurt me, I would react to her cruelty and defend myself.

"God was dealing with me for some time about my feelings toward my sister. I'm forty-five years old now. This has been going on for at least forty years. I finally heard Him telling me, 'You have to forgive her. It doesn't matter what she has done to you. It doesn't matter her response to you. I want you to love her in spite of her.'

"One day I just woke up and made up my mind to call my sister. I told her, 'You know what, sis? I am choosing now to walk in love toward you. And I am choosing to walk in forgiveness toward you, no matter how you feel about me.'

"I was shocked at my sister's response. She didn't exactly apologize to me for her behavior, but we talked for hours on that call. Now, believe it or not, after forty years of fighting we talk every day. I won't say that our relationship is perfect. When we talk I don't hesitate to say how I see things, and sometimes she'll come back with a zinger the way she used to. I just roll my eyes now and laugh about it. I don't react the way I did in the past. God has given me a renewed love for my sister.

"Shortly thereafter, God healed me of my smoking addiction. One morning I woke up and looked at my cigarettes. I was so disgusted. I said to God, 'I'm sick of smoking! If You will just help me, then I'm going to put these cigarettes down and never pick them up again.' That was several years ago, and I have been free of smoking ever since."

As I stood there listening to Mary, I was fascinated because I heard God speaking to me. My daughter has struggled with these same two issues – smoking and a strained relationship with her sister. God was telling me, "Don't ever give up. It can look as though it is going to continue forever. I can still repair broken relationships, and I can still deliver people from addictions."

I looked at Mary and said, "I am very interested in your testimony because I am concerned about my oldest daughter. She has these very same issues right now. Would you pray for her? Would you help me pray for my daughter?"

"Of course I will, Peggy. I'll add your daughter to my prayer list because I know that God is still in the miracle-working business. There is no relationship that has gone so wrong; there is no addiction so strong that He does not have the ability to help us conquer it."

If I had not opened my mouth to talk to people at work the way that I have done in this department, I never would have connected to these women the way that I have. We would not be sharing our challenges in life, or our love for the Lord, or the way He blesses us. Now I have church at work in between sales. It doesn't matter if I am giving or receiving words of encouragement and prayer. There is no question in my mind that I have been strategically placed in my job. There is also no question in my mind that God has orchestrated all the relationships I have made. Yes, I prayed for these women when they needed to hear from God. I also needed to hear from God, through Mary, for the challenges in my life. I needed to hear that God's grace has no limit. I needed reassurance to believe that even if I have not seen victory yet, I should not give up and think that victory will never come. I needed to be able to go home to tell my daughter, "Do you know that there is a woman at my work who is praying for you? She is telling me to tell you don't give up because there will be victory for you. You may have to wrestle some things to the ground, but you can push through this."

I had not seen Holly for a couple of weeks. Although she did not ask me to go with her to court, I remembered her court date and interceded for her that day. When I saw her again, she was absolutely glowing. She came over to hug me.

"Holly, I didn't want to disturb you at home, but I was going to send you a text message this week to ask how you're doing. I was praying for you when you were in court."

"Peggy, I felt it. I really felt it. You know, I went to church for the first time in a long while last Sunday. I went to the church where my babysitter takes my daughter when I am working on Sundays. My babysitter has been asking me for months to go to church with her. Do you remember how I told you that I felt as though I never grieved my divorce? I always just steeled myself for the sake of my child."

I nodded my head. I knew that feeling because I did that myself for years. When you're a single parent, everyone relies on you to be strong, so you cannot crumble. Even when there are daggers flying at you, you cannot show that they are penetrating your heart. Everyone else is looking to you to be the rock, but you are not the rock. Jesus is the Rock. You get into trouble whenever you try to be something that you were never meant to be. You begin to develop unrealistic expectations of yourself, and others do the same. Soon the cracks in the rock become crevasses, and you break.

"Well, I went up to the altar with my daughter. The pastors laid hands on me and prayed for me. I sobbed. I was weeping from deep inside of me. My daughter was looking at me a little concerned. She has never seen me cry like that. I had to explain to her that this was good crying. I was letting some bad feelings go and purging my soul.

"Peggy, there has been such a peace within me. We're not out of the woods, yet. We still have to go back to court, but you know, it's going to be okay. I still worry sometimes when my daughter goes to see her father because I'm concerned about the environment she may be in."

"Holly, I have two children who have been 1,600 miles away from me for years now. That used to tear me up. Then I started to realize that there is no time and space with God. I can pray and activate protection for them. I don't personally have to be there to fix everything. I used to go to sleep at night while my husband, Jim, would hold me as I cried myself to sleep. It would literally make me sick. I was especially afraid for my son, afraid that he was getting involved in potentially dangerous things in which he had no business. I was not there to try to speak truth into his life. He was not interested in what I had to say anyway.

"The truth is we can dispatch guardian angels when we pray. When you pray for your daughter, Angel, pray the protection of God over her. Thank Him for dispatching ministering and warring angels around her. Trust God with her. God will prove Himself to be faithful because He loves you. What you care about is what God cares about. When I pray for my children, I'm going to add Angel's name to my list."

"Oh, Peggy, would you?"

"Absolutely!"

"Thank you, Peggy."

There is power in prayer. There is power in agreement. We need to grasp the fact that we have the right to access the supernatural power of God because of the sacrifice of Jesus. God then assumes the responsibility. That concept can be hard for us to accept when we want to be there for our children. In a divorce, we cannot be there! One day we wake up and the children we used to see in our lives every day we now see only occasionally, if at all.

The natural instinct of parents to protect, to nurture, and to teach is still there. What can parents do with that instinct when their children are gone, even if temporarily? If it is not expressed, but stays inside them, it can torment them and cause depression. On the other hand, if they cry out to God, then He who sees all, knows all, and can do all takes up where their humanity leaves off. They can expect Him to do this. He promises that, if they commit their children to Him, He will be faithful to keep them. God already sees everything that is going on in every home. Nothing is hidden from Him. Those children cannot outrun Him. It is not always going to be easy, and their children may have to walk out their own journey. Sometimes they will wish their children did not have to suffer. At the end of it all, God promises He is faithful to bring everything full circle. Parents have to keep praying and trusting Him. They have to believe that He is sufficient when they are insufficient. Their sufficiency is in Christ.

Dear Daddy, I am grateful that I do not have to bear the burdens of my life alone. You are faithful to surround me with other believers who love You and love me. Together, we can stand and face whatever comes in life knowing that You hear us. Together, we present a formidable union in the face of darkness. We rejoice over one another's victories and weep over the sorrows. Your "church" is not a building. It is a living, vital organism. Corporate worship and instruction take place in our churches, but the structure was never meant to define us. I am thankful that Your Church of the Lord Jesus Christ is alive and functioning in me and around us. Wherever two or more of us are gathered in Your name together, there is "church". We can experience You and Your presence and Your power, anywhere, anytime.

Thank You for giving me victory over fear and intimidation. I am governed by the law of love. I respond with wisdom when I see someone who is suffering, anxious, and concerned. When I speak, Your words flow from my lips, which are anointed for encouragement and seasoned with mercy and grace. Teach me to develop relationships at work that will reflect Your care and concern for those around me. Teach me how to be a friend. Teach me how to protect the interests of others while I pursue success in my business affairs. This does not have to be mutually exclusive. I trust You to ground me wherever I may be. You are the Source. I do not have to fight or strive or vie for position or prominence. Help me to focus on being a blessing, and then You will take care of blessing me.

Thank You, Daddy, for hearing me. In Jesus' name, so be it. Amen.

Makeup Lesson 19: Eye Brow Color and Treatment

($) Your eyebrows are sisters, not twins. You can define a natural eyebrow shape with three points. Point A: Hold a pencil or handle of a brush vertically against the side of your nose and notice where it meets the brow. This is where the brow should begin. You can place a small dot of brow powder here for reference. Make sure you are looking directly ahead of you. Point B: Hold the pencil against your nostril and move it diagonally across the iris of the eye. Notice where the pencil meets the brow. This is the best place for the peak of your arch. You can place a small dot of powder here for reference. Point C: Again, place the pencil against your nostril, but this time, extend it diagonally to the outer corner of your eye. Where it meets the brow is the best place for your brow to end. The line should be thicker between A&B and thinner between B&C.

The goal in applying product is to mimic the natural brows. You want to apply in short, featherlike, hair strokes, never straight in a solid line. Simply dip a short, stiff-angled brush in the eye brow powder and apply it to the brows, starting at the arch of the brow as this will deposit the most color. The strokes should be used in the same direction as the hairs' natural growth.

Different product lines will carry a variety of brow applications. Some clients prefer a pencil; some prefer a wand that has a brush, which resembles a mascara brush. Whatever you prefer, the goal is to create a frame for the eyes. Eliminating any focus on the eyebrow is comparable to having a beautiful painting with no frame around it. Something about it appears incomplete.

Prior to any cosmetic approach, it is important to have eyebrows shaped. This can be accomplished by tweezing them to eliminate stray hairs from underneath the brow, or by having the eyebrows professionally waxed. The arch should be smooth and clean. They should not be too narrow.

Aging, certain drug therapies and hormonal imbalances all may cause the brows to thin. There are cosmetic treatments to address this but they are successful only if the hair follicle is not dead. If the follicle is just dormant, you will see a benefit. Begin now, if you have this issue.

Make sure the color of the eyebrow is complementary to your hair coloring.

Lesson #20

My Personal Makeover

Recently, I was in the restroom at work washing my hands. A customer there at the same time said to me, "Excuse me, you work here, don't you?"

"Yes, ma'am, I do," I replied as I dried my hands.

"I'll bet you work in the cosmetics department."

"Well, as a matter of fact, I do."

"I could tell. Your makeup is perfect. You are so beautiful!"

"Why, thank you! You're so kind," I replied, flattered.

The truth is that I get this kind of response from my clients almost every day. Honestly, I'm surprised every time I hear it, but it has happened to me so many times that my husband will ask me now when I come home, "Did anyone tell you today how beautiful you are?" He always expects me to say yes. I never received this many compliments about my looks when I was in my twenties or thirties. I thought I was past the age where I would get such unsolicited attention. Is it just the fact that I work in cosmetics, or is it something else?

At the cosmetics counter I provide several services. First, I educate clients about the science and the benefits of each product. At the same time, I analyze each woman's facial structure, the contour and coloring of her skin, as well as her particular skin concerns. Then, I recommend specific skin care systems and color products.

Second, I give makeup lessons in the art and application of cosmetic products to maximize a woman's assets and minimize her flaws. I teach each client how to use the same techniques I employ while she is sitting in my chair. It is not enough just to sell a product if the client goes home without knowing how to use it. Because of the ingredients in skin care products, there is a specific sequence when using them to maximize their effectiveness.

Finally, I do makeovers. This is a service I provide when a woman will come in before an event, such as a bridal party or a special date, and tell me she needs to be ready by a certain time. She is looking for help and wants my specific skills. She is not interested in my instruction. She is only interested in telling me what the event is and what colors she will be wearing. Then I just give her a makeover to get her ready.

Over the past year, I have also been giving makeup lessons about the Lord to my clients and coworkers using the Word of God and prayer. These products are in the Bible. Anyone can purchase a Bible, bring it home and let it sit on the shelf to collect dust. In the same way, any woman can purchase cosmetics, put them on her vanity and never use them. When a woman tries to read the Bible, she can find herself feeling intimidated, just as a woman who is not educated in the proper use of cosmetics may lack confidence to apply them herself. Spiritual confusion occurs when a woman has not learned to look at the written Word of God as an instruction manual, a paradigm for living. The Bible is a book filled with books that are divinely inspired and contain analogies and metaphors for contemporary living. When a woman learns to read the Bible and use it skillfully, it is the equivalent of buying a product, like cosmetics, which can alter your image. The more biblical instruction you take into yourself, and the more you put on the Word of God, the more you are recreated in the image of Christ. His likeness becomes your likeness.

During this same time, I have also been getting a spiritual makeover. I have just shown up, and God has done all the work. I have been in circumstances, and women have shared situations with me which were so overwhelming that there were no apparent answers at the moment. We would look at ourselves and acknowledge that we would never be able to heal from the personal wounds or scars unless God performed spiritual surgery on us. He had to do the work, as an expert plastic surgeon who knows how to cut away the deformities, or graft skin from another part of the body to make a scar smooth again.

We may never understand why certain experiences happen to us, or why people behave in certain ways. We have to trust God with the unknown. For example, I don't know why my sister, Bonnie, had an aneurism and drowned while she was swimming. I don't know why Cassie's sister was hit by a car and killed on that street corner just as Cassie rode up behind her. I don't know why men walk away from their wives and their children. I don't know why people kill, rape, and destroy. In this life I may never have answers to some of the very hurtful events which have happened to me or to those I love. We live in a fallen world. I do believe there is a heaven, and there will come a time when God will wipe away all tears from our eyes and pain from our hearts. I believe that when we see Him face to face, see Him as He is, and we know even as we are known, we will be too immersed in worshiping Him for the questions to matter anymore. All I can do now is show up and sit in the makeup chair and say to God, *"You see my scars. You see my wounds. You see the discoloration on me. Some patches on me are light, but some are dark. There are things I cannot fix on my own. I may not even be able to comprehend or process them. Father, You are going to have to do a makeover on me in order for me to function properly and to look like You."*

This is not just a cosmetic job. This is an inside spiritual work. The Holy Spirit is the only one who can perform this task. In the last year and a half that I have been getting my own spiritual makeover, I have seen myself engaged in all aspects of this dynamic. I have been a teacher with Debbie, who is in a situation similar to my first marriage which failed thirteen years before. I have also been a student. God gave me an exquisite picture of love in a covenant marriage when I met

Karen in the wheelchair. At other times, my clients have sat in the chair, and God has used me as an instrument of covering. I covered their hearts in prayer and friendship. In my friendship with Cassie, I shared with her the need to hear clearly from God, and let her know that I would stand with her regardless of the outcome.

In all these situations, the questions are the same. When the worst of life happens to me, is God real, or is He not? Is God sovereign, or is He not? Is God telling the truth, or is He a liar? What do I believe? Not, what do I *think* I believe, but what do I *really* believe?

If God is sovereign, then nothing that happens to me is a surprise to Him. If God is all powerful, then He can take the worst that happens to me and work it for my good and His glory. Nothing is beyond His ability to achieve. All things are indeed possible with God. If, in fact, He is the truth, then when He says, *"That I will never, never leave you. I will not, will not, will not. Assuredly not!"* I can take that and lay my head on the pillow at night. It does not matter if I believe the sky is falling. I can say, "God, someday, somewhere, somehow, You will make sense out of this for me. I trust You with my life. I cast all my cares upon You (1 Peter 5:7). I know You care for me. I have concluded that You are not a liar. You are all powerful, loving, and true. So no matter what happens, I can cast everything onto You. We are going to walk this out together. In the end, You and I will be victorious."

God also gives makeup lessons. When I was in school, I was able to take a makeup lesson if I got sick and missed a class. I got a second chance. What does that mean for me in my relationship with God? Maybe I needed to learn a lesson in life, but I was not willing to look at my own issues, or the issues of those around me. I was not willing to see what was in front of me. I was not willing to come to the chair, sit down, and remove my mask in order to be exposed and vulnerable. I never gave God a chance to reveal the solution that could have put my life on a different path. I have to be willing to sit in the chair. I have to be willing to admit that I cannot hide anything from Him. What do we think we are accomplishing by running from God? He knows exactly who we are and what is going on in our lives and our hearts. *"Lord ... You did form my inward parts; You did knit me together in my mother's womb... My frame was not hidden from You when I was being formed in secret, as if embroidered with various colors... Your eyes saw my unformed substance, and in Your book all the days of my life were written before ever they took shape..."* (Psalm 139: 13, 15-16).

It breaks the heart of God and diminishes our potential when we fail to submit ourselves to the process of being conformed to the image of Christ. The Word of God says, *"Do not be conformed to this world, fashioned after and adapted to its external, superficial customs, but be transformed by the renewal of your mind"* (Romans 12:2). This is the ultimate makeup lesson. Sometimes God will sit me in the chair to tell me that I am messing up in life because I do not know what I am doing. God says, *"My people are destroyed for lack of knowledge"* (Hosea 4:6).

Some well-meaning people may intellectually submit to the teaching of their religious leaders, but miss the application of the lessons in the Word of God. They can go through life never understanding that in the Bible God has defined a way for a husband to treat his wife, *"Husbands, love your wives, as Christ loved the church and gave Himself up for her"* (Ephesians 5:25); a way for parents to raise children, *"Train up a child in the way he should go, and when he is old he will not depart from it"* (Proverbs 22:6); and a way for people to handle their money, *"'Bring all the tithes (the whole tenth of your income) into the storehouse, that there may be food in My house, and prove Me now by it,' says the Lord of hosts, 'if I will not open the windows of heaven for you and pour you out a blessing, that there shall not be room enough to receive it'"* (Malachi 3:10). For all conflicts in life, God has provided a solution. If they never learn how to take the product, the Word of God, and skillfully apply it, they may become frustrated and conclude that this Christian walk does not work, and decide that a Christian life is ineffective.

When I have failed in my life to apply the Word of God skillfully, He has given me a makeup lesson. I hit the wall. I became convicted and could no longer hide it. I was finally willing to submit myself to a friend, and to the Holy Spirit, and say, "I am willing for you to see my wounds." In order to be healed, I had to be willing to be authentic and genuine. Not only did I have to take the makeup lesson, I also had to invest in the product and wear it. I had to put on the full armor of God in order to withstand the attacks of the enemy (Ephesians 6:11-18). I had to wear love, kindness, and forgiveness. If I was not willing to wear the Word of God, then it was never going to have any value or do me any good. In the makeup lessons of my life, I had to be willing to participate and be obedient to the Holy Spirit.

I can now see how the events in my life are connected. Through the tough times, I had a choice to trust God, believing that He does all things well. His timing is perfect. He may tarry, but He is never late. He knows exactly what He is doing. Working in retail, returning to Westlake, Louisiana, and singing in my New Jersey high school were clearly examples of God's plan for my life. These events happened to me. I never saw them coming. God picked me up and took me back to places where I had been years before. Through these experiences I could hear God telling me, *"I was with you then, as I am with you now. Nothing in your life is disconnected. I will work all things together for good."*

I can think of no more dramatic example of God's perfect timing and my personal makeover than my relationship and involvement with a woman and former neighbor in my childhood neighborhood, Rosemarie D'Alessandro. I grew up in Hillsdale, New Jersey. Across the street from the house where I lived was the D'Alessandro family – Frank and Rosemarie and their children, Frankie, Marie, and Joan. When I was fifteen, I would occasionally babysit the children. Joan was seven years old.

One spring afternoon on Holy Thursday, Joan skipped down the steps of her home to go sell Girl Scout cookies in the neighborhood. She went over to the home of a local high school teacher, Joseph McGowan. Joan never came home. Joseph McGowan raped this little girl and brutally murdered her in his basement. Later that evening, he took Joan's battered little body in the trunk of his car up to New York and dumped it in Harriman State Park. Later, McGowan helped in the initial search for Joan. Joan's body was found on Easter Sunday. Before long, McGowan became a suspect and failed a lie detector test. Eventually, he was tried, found guilty and sentenced to life in prison. According to the existing sentencing guidelines in New Jersey, which were consistent with other states, McGowan would be eligible for parole in seven to fourteen years. The possibility existed that a man convicted of the sexual assault and murder of a child would serve no more than seven years.

This was a possibility which Joan's mother, Rosemarie, could not allow. Rosemarie has worked tirelessly for the last forty years to change the sentencing laws in this country so that any person convicted of the murder and sexual assault of a child would never be eligible for parole.

In 1998, President Clinton signed a federal version of Joan's law which imposes a life sentence without the possibility of parole. To date, only New York and New Jersey have adopted this version. Furthermore, the law in New Jersey is not retroactive. Every time McGowan comes up for parole, Rosemarie is there to testify against his eligibility. Every time she testifies, she has to remind herself of the horrible way McGowan raped her daughter and beat her skull. So far, she has been successful in preventing McGowan's release on parole.

Based on Rosemarie's work to change the sentencing laws and honor her daughter's memory by establishing the Joan D'Alessandro Memorial Foundation, I identified Rosemarie as one of the Steel Magnolias I wanted to feature in an episode of my series. Then on September 7, 2013, which would have been Joan's forty-seventh birthday, Rosemarie hosted a celebration for her daughter and a fundraiser for the Joan D'Alessandro Memorial Foundation. Rosemarie asked me to come and speak at the event. This meant going back to my home town where I would visit with her. She still lived in the same house she did when Joan was murdered, and could still look across the street to see McGowan's old house. I assembled a team to work with me to create a documentary called, *Joan The Angel Advocate*. My goal was to highlight Joan's story and to create a useful tool for people in other states who want to get involved in changing the sentencing laws for child murderers in their state.

I never knew when I was fifteen years old that one day I would be a producer. Why did I live on that street? Why was I Joan's babysitter? I never knew that my neighbor was going to murder this little girl. I never knew then that I would possess a set of skills and a voice that could help Rosemarie in her quest for justice and to change the laws of the country. Is this just a random coincidence? No, I believe it was all part of a plan, even though there was no evidence of the plan until forty years later.

It seemed that everywhere I went that year the number forty was chasing me. In Scripture, the number forty indicates transition. The plan was unfolding in front of me. I was not making it up. It was God's plan. I was showing up, and He was executing the plan. I just stepped back and marveled. Who would have thought that forty years later God would knit the threads of my life together as He has? Now when I look back, I do not see it as a knotted mess on the backside of the tapestry. I'm not saying that my life is perfect. It's not finished yet, but God is allowing me to flip the tapestry over to see how He is weaving all the different parts together. He is transforming me into the Peggy image of Jesus on earth.

Your image has your name on it and is a reflection of Him through your life. It looks different from my image. God wants to use you to reveal His Kingdom work in the world. The Kingdom of God is revealed as righteousness, peace, and joy in the Holy Ghost. You and I are assigned to bring these things into this world. God loves you as much as He loves me, because He is no respecter of persons. The image and purpose for your life are just as outstanding and significant to Him and to the world.

To realize your own transformation, you are going to have to show up, take the mask off, and sit in the chair. You may have to reveal your flaws to another believer, a pastor, or godly counselor and say, just like the consultants in the cosmetics department, "Would you pray with me?" No one can pray for you effectively if you are not transparent. If you appear in life as though you have got it all together, with your image firmly in place, even though you are shattered underneath, no one will have access to the real you. Fear is the root of your isolation. You can overcome this fear by understanding that there is no fear in love (1 John 4:18). God unconditionally loves and accepts you.

Seven years ago, there was a two-month period in my life when I was suffering from adrenal exhaustion. In the mornings, I would move from my bed to the couch and could barely get up to take care of myself. I did not know what was happening to me. I was emotionally, physically, and financially depleted. All day long I would sit on the couch, turn on the television and watch one ministry show after another. This was God's way of spiritually feeding me when I was broken and beaten down. When my husband would come home, I would tell him about the wonderful insights I received that day from the Lord. I know at times he was frustrated with me, but he would simply ask, "What did you hear today at the Church of the Holy Couch?" I needed God to reveal Himself to me and perform a makeover on me. That is when I sat in His chair. He began to transform me by renewing my mind. This gave me the ability to heal from past hurts and face difficult circumstances years later without falling apart. Armed with His perspective, I would see future trials as stepping stones to spiritual victory.

I do not know what circumstances you face at this moment. I will tell you that the love of God is so profound and all-encompassing that He will run to meet you wherever you are. Allow him to touch your face and anoint you with oil, touch your lips, and change the words that come out of your mouth. He will teach you how to pray and say words of encouragement that manifest the fruit of the spirit - love, gentleness, meekness, joy, kindness, patience, goodness, longsuffering and self-control. (Galatians 5:22-23). Let him treat your eyes, so that you begin to open them to His Word. Be willing to listen and pay attention to how you look and sound to others. Be willing to take the product and use it. Be willing to yield yourself to Christ knowing full well that He is an expert artist. His goal is that you will reflect His glory in your life. You do not have to be afraid. When you sit in the chair, He strips off your mask and looks at you. You will not see your shame in His eyes. You will not see God wince with disgust when He looks at you. The truth is that He will be so delighted that you have chosen to trust Him, and to sit down and reveal what you have hidden from the rest of the world for so long.

Give God a chance to fix what you cannot fix yourself. He can reverse the damage to your soul caused by the choices you have made in life, or by the unfair actions of other people. You can either hide or submit. Your choice will determine the direction of the rest of your life. When you set aside time for prayer and worship, He will reveal Himself to you. Then not only will you start to experience richness in your spiritual life, you will also start to walk in the abundant life for which Jesus died to give you.

In the beginning, I considered going back to work at the makeup department as my personal failure. Since then, I have become convinced that success is not the source of happiness. My dreams for a successful future in my field were only temporarily delayed by betrayal and loss. I found true joy from being in the will of God at the makeup counter. My love for the women in my department grew as I understood that God was using the circumstances of my journey as a teaching tool to show me His purpose for my life.

My makeover is ongoing. Your makeover will be ongoing as well. As women age, we use different products. The expectations are different. The results are different. At each age, however, a woman can be beautiful. The spirit of a maturing woman can shine brighter than what you may see physically. As her life becomes a reflection of the greatness of God and His manifestation in her life, she achieves greatness. The Word says, *"But whenever a person turns in repentance to the Lord, the veil is stripped off and taken away. Now the Lord is the Spirit, and where the Spirit of the Lord is, there is emancipation from bondage and freedom. And all of us, as with unveiled face, continued to behold as in a mirror the glory of the Lord, are constantly being transfigured into His very own image in ever increasing splendor and from one degree of glory to another"* (2 Corinthians 3:16-18). The more we mature in Christ, the more our face and our lives shine with the glory of the Lord. I believe this has been happening to me. I see it happening also to the women around me.

My prayer is that the stories in this book have enriched and encouraged you. Yes, I have included practical makeup lessons in each chapter both to have fun and help you become the best you can be physically. More importantly, I pray that going forward you will embrace His makeup lessons, and not be afraid to sit in the chair. Trust Him and He will transform your life into a reflection of Jesus. When He is finished and holds up the mirror before you, all you will be able to do is sit back and say with marvelous excitement, "Look at what the Lord has done! Praise God! Together, we made it to the other side!"

"Through many dangers, toils and snares
I have already come;
'Tis Grace that brought me safe thus far
and Grace will lead me home."

John Newton, "Amazing Grace", 1779

Dear Daddy, thank You for all You have done in my life, and all that You will continue to do. You have used the joys and the agonies, the friends and the enemies, as well as the peaks and the valleys to shape me into Your likeness. I recognize that You are not finished yet. Forgive me for kicking at the process. You know what You are doing. You are the potter, and I am indeed the clay.

As I look at this complex tapestry, which is my life, I acknowledge that there are no loose ends with You. When I am frustrated because I do not understand, I rest in Your arms and wait patiently for You to complete the work You have begun in me. You promised that You would. Unlike man, You never go back on Your Word.

I am not a victim. You promise that I will have victory over everything in my life. As I acknowledge Your hand in my past, I fully trust that You will be involved in every aspect of my future. There is nothing about me that You do not know. There is no suffering or obstacle too great in my life that You and I cannot overcome together. Give me the discipline and the character to yield to the voice of the Holy Spirit in my life. Help me to be as patient with others as You have been with me.

Thank you for teaching me to sing in the storm and dance in the rain. I have learned to do that by faith, not by feeling. You are teaching me to see myself, others, and events in my life through Your eyes. When I ask You for this revelation knowledge, You are faithful to bring me higher. Everything looks so much different from where You sit.

I do not know where the road leads. I can only see so far. It is enough for me that You see for me. You are my faithful friend. You are my safe harbor. You are my gallant prince. You are my protective warrior. You are my All in all.

Tomorrow, when I wake up in the morning, we will begin my lessons again. Whatever You apply will serve to make me more beautiful in Your eyes.

In Jesus' name, so be it! Amen.

Makeup Lesson 20: Fragrances

($$$) There are so many fragrances on the market that it can be time consuming to choose the one you like best. Designers, celebrities, and prestige lines all have signature fragrances. I have several that I like. What I wear depends on what mood I am in, where I am going, or the season of the year. My husband has a particular fragrance that he loves for me to wear.

In choosing a fragrance, it is important to understand the idea of layering. During the holidays, each fragrance will typically sell a boxed gift set. This will include the fragrance, either eau de toilette or eau de parfum, shower body gel, body lotion, and perhaps some body powder. It is typically less expensive to purchase these items in a set than independently.

Start layering by showering with the gel. After the shower when the body is still warm and a bit moist, use the body lotion. Afterwards, if you like, use the powder. Spray the fragrance on the back of your knees, and other places where your pulse is located.

By layering, you not only nourish the skin with the lotion and dry the skin with the powder, you actually use less of the expensive spray. The fragrance will also remain noticeable on your skin. You will end up using less of the most expensive item.

When you are considering a new fragrance, sales consultants will gladly offer samples. This is important because everyone's body chemistry is different. Some fragrances may smell wonderfully on someone else, and quite different on you. Certain fragrances tend to last longer than others.

In choosing a fragrance, the consultant should be able to tell you what the top notes are. I have always thought this to be a very clinical approach. I am less concerned with what is in it, unless I fear an allergic reaction, and more concerned with how it fits my style and personality.

Bible Study

Bibliography

1. *Steel Magnolias*, directed by Herbert Ross, TriStar Pictures, 1989
2. *The Horse Whisperer*, directed by Robert Redford, Buena Vista Pictures,1998
3. Batterson, Mark. *The Circle Maker*, Zondervan, 2012
4. Lucado, Max. *The Applause of Heaven*, Thomas Nelson, 2011
5. *The Princess Diaries 2: Royal Engagment,* directed by Garry Marshall, Buena Vista Pictures, 2004
6. Tomlin, Diane. *The Secret Holocaust Diaries,* Tyndale House Publishers, 2010
7. The Stoning of Soraya M., directed by Cyrus Nowrasteh, Roadside Attractions, 2008

My Scrapbook

I hope you have enjoyed these makeup lessons. Now it's your turn. You will see that this section includes blank pages so that you may create your own scrapbook as described in Lesson #10. Write your own thoughts, or capture personal stories of encounters with people in your life. Then share them with your family, your friends, and even your co-workers. See how God begins to bless you.

Start by including some pictures of yourself before you read this book. Put these pictures in the beginning of your journal. After reading this book, spending some time in prayer, journaling, and getting a makeover yourself, take some new pictures of yourself and include them at the end of your journal. Of course, you may also share your pictures and stories on the Facebook page at MakeupLessonsTheBook.

Here are some questions and situations you may want to consider in your own journal:

1. What does the tapestry of your life look like today? Can you praise Him in all things?
2. How has God shown you that He cares about the smallest details of your life?
3. Is it difficult or hard for you to trust God? Why?
4. Have you ever had to serve someone with opinions and a lifestyle different from yours?
5. Do you see your life as going backward or forward?
6. How much has legalistic thinking dominated your spiritual life? Are you able to free yourself?
7. When and how have you received a word from God?
8. Is there anything in your life that you are afraid to reveal?
9. Describe the dreams and visions for your life. What price would you pay to achieve them?
10. Write the prayers you and your partners pray together. Circle the promises you are claiming.
11. What are the desires of your heart?
12. Describe situations which rob you of your peace. How could you maintain your peace?
13. Are you comfortable in your own skin? Why or why not?
14. Describe a second chance opportunity you have had or would like to have.
15. Describe opportunities you have or have had to intercede for others in crisis.
16. Write a letter of encouragement to someone. Share it with them personally.
17. Describe a married couple whom you admire. Do they have a covenant relationship?
18. Describe how God has blessed you.
19. Has fear interfered with an uplifting, intimate relationship in your life? How?
20. Describe how you know that God is real.
21. What part of your life needs a makeover?

Makeup Palettes

The following pages have outlines of the face, the eyes, and the lips. I have included them in this book so that you can take them with you to any makeup consultant. As you get a makeover, the consultant can put the same colors on these outlines so that you can see how to apply the colors at home. Remember this tip when applying lip color to the outline. Ask the makeup consultant to put clear plastic tape over the lip color so that it doesn't bleed onto the previous page.

There are four copies so that you can create four different looks, one for each season of the year, for example. Don't worry about spending a lot of money on makeup to create all these looks at one time. Go step by step, or season by season. Add products as you can. Be sure to ask the consultant for the dates of the next "gift with purchase" and "purchase with purchase" promotions. Record these dates for each season and remind yourself to take advantage of the promotions in order to save money. Have fun!

Look for updates from me at www.facebook.com/MakupLessonsTheBook.

SPRING Look:

Makeup consultant: ______________________________

Location: ______________________________

Phone: ______________ Email: ______________

Next Gift with Purchase: ________ Next Purchase with Purchase: ________

NOTES:

Brand	Name	Number/Type/Purpose	Color

SUMMER Look:

Makeup consultant: ____

Location: ____

Phone: ______________________ Email: ______________________________

Next Gift with Purchase: ____________ Next Purchase with Purchase: _________

NOTES:

Brand	Name	Number/Type/Purpose	Color

FALL Look:

Makeup consultant: ______________________________

Location: ______________________________

Phone: ______________ Email: ______________

Next Gift with Purchase: __________ Next Purchase with Purchase: __________

NOTES:

Brand	Name	Number/Type/Purpose	Color

WINTER Look:

Makeup consultant: ______________________________

Location: ______________________________

Phone: ______________ Email: ______________

Next Gift with Purchase: __________ Next Purchase with Purchase: __________

NOTES:

Brand	Name	Number/Type/Purpose	Color